ONLY HUMAN

Christian Reflections on
the Journey Toward Wholeness

David P. Gushee

Foreword by
Stanley Hauerwas

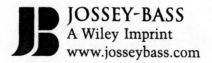

JOSSEY-BASS
A Wiley Imprint
www.josseybass.com

Published by Jossey-Bass
A Wiley Imprint
989 Market Street, San Francisco, CA 94103-1741   www.josseybass.com

Jossey-Bass books and products are available through most bookstores.
To contact Jossey-Bass directly call our Customer Care Department within the
U.S. at 800-956-7739, outside the U.S. at 317-572-3986, or fax 317-572-4002.

Jossey-Bass also publishes its books in a variety of electronic formats. Some content that
appears in print may not be available in electronic books.

Credits appear on p. 224.

Library of Congress Cataloging-in-Publication Data
Gushee, David P., date
  Only human : Christian reflections on the journey toward wholeness /
David P. Gushee ; foreword by Stanley Hauerwas.—1st ed.
      p. cm.—(Enduring questions in Christian life series)
  Includes bibliographical references and index.

  1. Self-actualization (Psychology)—Religious aspects—Christianity.
2. Christian life. 3. Christianity—Philosophy. I. Title. II. Series.
  BV4598.2.G87 2005
  248.4—dc22   2005008650
ISBN: 978-0-470-88961-9

FIRST EDITION
HB Printing   10 9 8 7 6 5 4 3 2 1

ONLY
HUMAN

The
ENDURING QUESTIONS
IN CHRISTIAN LIFE™
Series

Enduring Questions in Christian Life™ is a series of books designed to speak intelligently and intelligibly to the deepest spiritual and moral concerns of Christians and thoughtful seekers. The title of the series reflects its purpose: to offer Christian reflection on questions that are significant not just for Christians but for all people. This series seeks to offer thoughtful, compassionate, and provocative explorations of essential matters that arise at the intersection of faith and life. We hope that this series will provide practical guidance for thinking about particular issues in a complex and changing world while opening the reader to a deeper appreciation of the rich direction for life's journey that is available in historic Christian thought. Books in the series seek to be informed by the best in theological reflection, to address enduring questions in new and graceful ways, to avoid polemics, and to jar readers out of old patterns of thinking about life's most significant issues.

Volumes in the Enduring Questions in Christian Life™ Series are designed to speak to those who are unlikely to read (or even find) technical works in Christian theology or ethics but are open to thoughtful reflections that reach both head and heart and help people discern how they are supposed to live this life. The books represent a variety of distinctive faith traditions, but all are ecumenical enough to attract rather than repel seekers and those who come from different strands of Christian tradition. The Enduring Questions in Christian Life™ Series aims to embody a graceful combination of sober consideration of the human condition and hope in God. Amid the whirl of daily events and the carnage of the daily headlines, the series calls readers into a tradition of Christian reflection that can account adequately both for that carnage and for the hope that gets the last word.

David P. Gushee
Series Editor

CONTENTS

Contents

FOREWORD

I n this wonderful book Dave Gushee helps us understand what a difficult task it is to be "only human." The very humanity that constitutes our "only" cannot resist the temptation to be more than human. We cannot resist trying to be more than human because we are so frightened of being human. We are so because as creatures created by a good God, we fear our very creatureliness.

Perhaps no event in our time has revealed our desire to be more than human more than the American response to September 11, 2001. Americans quite simply are now a people ruled by fear. We want to be more than human, securing safety that simply cannot be secured in the world as we know it. As a result, we impose injustice on other people in the interests of securing ourselves from suffering and death.

Gushee helps us see that our attempts to be more than human must be called by the name we so desperately desire to avoid, that is: sin. To be human requires we confess that though we are creatures of a good God, created to desire and love God, we turn away from God, alienating ourselves from one another and, ironically, from our own lives. Moreover, we discover that we cannot will our way out of sin, but rather we can only recover our humanity by accepting the gifts we receive from others made possible by God.

This is a book in theological anthropology, and that is a great achievement. Often books that are about "being human" are more about us than about God. Gushee, however, beautifully develops an account of what it means for us to be embodied creatures, unintelligible if we do not see how our lives are constituted by the story God has made possible through the calling of the People of Israel and the life, death, and resurrection of Jesus Christ. This is a wise book, drawing on the wisdom of the Scripture to illumine who we are in a way that helps us better live as human beings.

But as I observed, it's not easy to be only human. Gushee, however, has the gift of the apposite example and remark that helps us discover what it means to be only human. For example, I am a deeply committed cat lover. Gushee seems also to know a good deal about cats, reminding us that we share a great deal with cats. Indeed, as humans we share more in common with cats than we do with God. After all, humans and cats are both creatures created to glorify God. However, Gushee helps us see as committed cat lovers that our love of cats draws us beyond our commonality with cats to the love that God has shown toward us by becoming one of us in Jesus Christ.

One of the other extraordinary features of this book is Gushee's familiarity with a wide range of traditions. In particular, he draws on the wisdom of the Catholic tradition to help us understand how important habituation is for being only human. Through the acquisition of habits, character is developed that makes us capable of being humane. Gushee then develops exemplifications of that humanity by calling attention to the lives of Wilberforce, Nightingale, and

Bonhoeffer. What a wonderful way to end a book on anthropology by giving us examples of what it means to be "only human."

Finally, this is a book that hopefully will exemplify a mode of theological writing we so desperately need. Without in any way avoiding the complexity of theological issues, Gushee has written a book that is readable. It is not only readable; it is inviting. I think anyone picking up this book will soon discover they are pulled from page to page simply because they find the writing at once engaging and profound. What a promising beginning for the series Dave Gushee is editing, "Enduring Questions in Christian Life." May his tribe increase.

Stanley Hauerwas

To my parents,
Dave and Jay Gushee—
wise guides on life's journey

ACKNOWLEDGMENTS

This is a different kind of book for me and so it has required a different kind of writing and editing process. By training I am a Christian ethicist, which basically means that I teach the principles and applications of Christian morality. Most of my books have been written specifically about ethical issues and often at a pretty technical level.

This book is about theology, not ethics. Better, it's about human life as we all experience it, and the contribution that Christian thought can make to understanding this life. In particular, my topic is human nature, what it means to be human and how we can understand ourselves and those around us as we all progress on the journey toward—well, toward whatever we understand wholeness or the good life to be.

This is a book not for specialists, but for anybody who has ever wondered what life is all about and what is going on inside us as we live it. Therefore in the writing process I have sought counsel primarily from people who, in my view, exhibit wisdom and insight about life itself.

It is these people that I wish to thank here, even while exonerating them of any errors, especially theological errors, that might be found here.

The original idea for a book about human nature emerged out of a conversation with two dear colleagues of mine at Union University, Jimmy Davis and Hal Poe. My thanks to them for allowing me to run off with the idea in my own direction. They continue to do fruitful work in this area as well.

Thanks to my sister Janette Laughlin; my mother-in-law, Earlynn Grant; and my friends Tom Shoe and Chad Davis for reading every word of this book and bringing to the reading their own unique gifts. Thanks to my colleague Barbara Perry and student Brian Wells for reviewing the manuscript as well.

Sheryl Fullerton, my editor at Jossey-Bass, has blessed my life richly. I am so grateful to her, not just for the insightful line-by-line editing that has made this book so much better than it otherwise would have been, but for our friendship as it has blossomed over the years that we have worked together toward the launch of this new series, Enduring Questions in Christian Life. I so much look forward to seeing the fruit of our shared labors in the years to come. Thanks for seeing something in me that I never knew was there, Sheryl.

This book is dedicated to my parents, David E. Gushee and Jay Gushee of Front Royal, Virginia. Of course, I will always think of them not in their Front Royal home but in the Vienna, Virginia, home in which they raised me. It was around that dinner table and watching them that I learned most of whatever wisdom I may have acquired through the years. It seems more than appropriate that it was their review of this manuscript and their suggestion that led to the decision to work intensively with the image of life as a journey toward wholeness. It's just fitting that two people who often spoke of life in rich metaphors around the dinner table should be the ones to come up with the ruling metaphor of this book. Mom and Dad, this book is dedicated to you, and that dedication is richly deserved, for yours has been a well-trod journey indeed.

Jackson, Tennessee   David P. Gushee
June 2005

Life's Journey, Human Nature, and the Quest for Wholeness

The path of the righteous is like the light of dawn,
which shines brighter and brighter until full day.
—PROVERBS 4:18

We got the call at home around 11:00 P.M. that a friend of ours from church had just put forty painkillers into her stomach in an effort to kill herself. The ambulance was on the scene.

I tracked Cindy (not her real name) down at a local motel and reached her by phone. I overheard the paramedics in the background. I asked her why she had done this. In her fuzzy voice, Cindy said, "Why does everyone always ask me questions like that? You wouldn't understand." Before the conversation could get much further, she was carted away to the hospital.

No, I wouldn't understand. I didn't understand. Despite many years in school, many years in ministry, and many years in life, I still do not really understand why people take bottles of pills and try to end their lives. Of course I know that

1

there is a sophisticated science of human psychology—actually, many sciences, many philosophies, many theories of human health, wholeness, and well-being—but there remains an impenetrable mystery to the act of dumping a bottle of pills down one's throat. Despite all that we know about chemical imbalances, depression, and so on, such an act can never be fully understood by anyone's science, anyone's theory.

It would be a whole lot safer to leave the discussion there—out there, away from *me*, away from us *healthy people,* out there with those sick people, people other than me. *Their* behavior is a mystery, not mine. I am normal. My behavior makes perfect sense. Right?

But there was much about my own behavior, and about my own attitudes and emotions, that bewildered me that night. It turns out that I will need to tell you the rest of the story.

Cindy is a woman in her mid-fifties who was shattered by the abuse she received in childhood at the hands of her father, who happened to be a Christian minister. She has never fully recovered. At the time of her suicide attempt, Cindy had for a decade been a member of the church in which I shared pastoral duties at the time. Cindy has had trouble maintaining steady employment and therefore a steady place to live. At the time she tried to kill herself, she was actually staying in our home. I knew she was struggling, but when she informed us that she was going away for a few days, I was secretly more relieved than worried. I had been struggling to feel compassion for Cindy this time around. She had stayed with us before, and I was concerned that this stay was not going well, was going to last too long, was going to disrupt the routines of my family of five (myself, my wife, kids aged fifteen, thirteen, and eleven), and was going to ask more of us than we were ready or willing to give.

Even when I heard that she had taken the pills, I struggled to find compassion. I knew what I was supposed to feel, as a Christian, as a human being—but the sparks were faint. My spirit was weary. My ongoing burdens at work and home were very heavy, as usual, because of my tendency to get overcommitted as I chase whatever dreams I am chasing. I was sick with a nagging cold. And all of that managed to distract me from actually caring that a human being staying in our home, a member of my church flock, a sacred person made in the image of God, had nearly ended her life in a cheap motel room down the street.

I was disgusted with myself. That night I did not sleep well. Thoughts of Cindy, and of my own indifference, perturbed me. In my restlessness, I sensed God poking me to *feel* again and to *act* again in a manner more consistent with the beliefs I hold most dear. The faint embers of compassion—and of nearness to God—began to stir once more.

This is a book about human nature and the way that who we are as beings affects how we journey through our lives. Our journeys as human beings begin in childhood and extend to and even beyond death. As we grow toward adulthood, we are expected to take greater and greater control of our own progress. Most of us gain some greater knowledge of who we are—our strengths and weaknesses, inborn talents, predilections—and put that together with what we have been taught and have learned about life to create a deeper understanding of what constitutes "success" or "wholeness" and therefore what destination we should pursue and how to get there. But along the way, we encounter many perplexing moments and questions, when who we thought we were (and who we thought others were), as well as how we believe we should behave, become mysterious. Why have I chosen the path I have while my friend Cindy, who tried to kill herself, chose such a different route through life? Is it all about me, who I am and how I have learned to live, or are there other factors—inborn and learned—that play an equally large role in the paths we choose and our progress along them? Which ingredient in who I am is most important? What can I change? What can't I? This is a book for those who have similar questions about what it means to be human and are seeking a clearer sense of direction for life's journey—and perhaps surer terrain on which to travel.

The premise of the biblical wisdom tradition and of the Christian tradition that has incorporated it and elaborated on it over the course of two thousand years is that God created human beings and in doing so also graciously charted a path for living the one life he has given us. Life's journey will culminate in success, according to the Christian faith, only if it is undertaken according to the path that God has established for it. This passage from Proverbs expresses this understanding especially well:

> My child, do not forget my teaching,
> But let your heart keep my commandments;
> For length of days and years of life
> And abundant welfare they will give you.
> Do not let loyalty and faithfulness forsake you;
> Bind them around your neck,
> Write them on the tablet of your heart.
> So you will find favor and good repute
> In the sight of God and of people.
> Trust in the Lord with all your heart,
> And do not rely on your own insight.

In all your ways acknowledge him,
And he will make straight your paths.
Do not be wise in your own eyes;
Fear the Lord and turn away from evil.
It will be a healing for your flesh
And a refreshment for your body.
—PROVERBS 3:1–8

Many of us attempt to chart our own course and in so doing almost invariably end up in a ditch somewhere (or in quicksand or on rocky shoals or over a cliff or in a pool of fiery lava—choose your own favorite image of personal disaster; all are appropriate). Eventually, if we are fortunate enough to have the chance to dust ourselves off and deal with the mess we have made, it is hard for us to avoid the conclusion that wherever the path that leads to "life," true and joyful life, may lie, we have not been on it. And maybe, just maybe, we would like to stop stumbling into ditches and find a better path once and for all.

This is a book for those who are at least open to considering the wisdom that remains available within the Christian tradition for navigating life's journey. It is the first in a series of books that is aimed at accomplishing the same purpose: serving readers by helping them discover the great riches for life's journey that are available within historic Christian thought. Perhaps you have tried other options and found them inadequate. Or perhaps you are a Christian but want to understand more clearly what being a Christian means in finding direction for life's journey.

In order to journey safely and successfully to your destination, you need a clear sense of where you're going, directions on how to get there, some sense of hazards and challenges you may meet along the way, and whether your equipment is up to the task. When it comes to navigating life's journey, the Christian tradition offers insights concerning all four of these elements. It does not speak with a single voice, but taken as a whole, it does offer a kind of guidance that has directed the paths of many millions of people over the centuries. This book addresses primarily that fourth element—our equipment for the journey, our human nature, considered through a Christian lens.

Although all four elements are important, the nature of the human being attempting to make life's journey is the logical starting point, in part because the issues involved in understanding human nature are so difficult. Figuring out how we as human beings work and how we successfully journey from birth to eternity is infinitely more complicated than grasping the specifications of even the most complex vehicles for an actual cross-country journey. My three-year-old daughter once amazed me by saying, "People are a miracle, Daddy." She was certainly right. But people are also a mess. We can't really figure out how to navigate life's journey without thinking pretty deeply about this miraculous mess that is human nature and how to properly make the trip. Other than the question of God, the question of human nature is the grandest and most perplexing on the planet. To help us find our way in life's journey, I want to pose questions about what it means to be a human being, about our makeup and our nature, about what is right and what is wrong with us, about our origins and our destiny—and about the God who is the source of our life.

To ask such questions is to join a discussion that has been going on throughout recorded history. We are a mystery to ourselves, our behavior inspiring and yet horrifying, our motives comprehensible and yet perplexing, our nature exalted and yet debased. No civilization lacks the evidence of struggle with these questions, for they go to the core of who we are as individuals, what kinds of communities we create, what problems we continually face, what possibilities we dream of, and what fears most beset us.

In this book, I will take on eight questions that I find most compelling in wrestling with the mystery of human nature and its impact on life's journey:

Is there such a thing as human nature, something all
   humans share?

How do we understand what we are made of?

Why do relationships matter so much to us?

Is it true that human beings are intrinsically sinful?

Are human beings truly free to chart their own path and
   make meaningful choices?

How do we become morally good people—or for that
   matter, morally evil ones?

What does a morally great life look like?

What should we hope for as our ultimate goal for life's
   journey?

I write this book as one human being to others. I write out of the same gnawing perplexity that, I hope, motivates you as a reader to pick up this book and others like it. I want to make progress in penetrating the mystery of my own self and how to live this journey and in so doing help you make progress in penetrating that mystery for yourself. My main qualification for writing this book is that I am a fellow human traveler who has thought quite a bit about the questions all of us face. I write not from above the human condition but very much from within.

In wrestling with such questions, I have been open to learning from anyone who has something true to say about the issues we are considering here. But as I have already indicated, the approach I am taking here is a Christian one. To some extent this is simply unavoidable because I am a Christian scholar and pastor and have been trained to think in classic Christian ways. My thought is governed and disciplined by biblical teaching as interpreted in the classic, orthodox Christian tradition of two millennia. But I stand within this tradition not by default but because I believe it to be truthful and wise. I think that the insights offered within the best of the Christian intellectual tradition are like nuggets of gold. They are valuable, they are enduring, they have stood the test of time, and they continue to gleam. Join me as we explore life's journey and the nature of the human creatures who undertake it.

1

Does "Human Nature" Even Exist?

Man has no nature; what he has is history.
— JOSE ORTEGA Y GASSET (1935)

A Milwaukee man named Jeffrey Dahmer very much enjoyed luring young men into his apartment, torturing them, killing them, cooking them, and eating them.

An Albanian nun called Mother Teresa spent her life serving the poor, sick, and dying. She gained her greatest satisfaction in representing the love of Jesus to the wretched of the earth. As she served them, she said, she saw Jesus in their battered and suffering bodies.

William Wilberforce devoted much of his adult life to abolishing the slave trade in England. He believed that slavery was an evil institution that must be destroyed. He heard the news of the success of his forty-five-year crusade on his deathbed.

During the very moments in which Wilberforce was offering his most moving speeches to Parliament, some slavemasters throughout the Western Hemisphere were branding, whipping, torturing, and killing their suffering captives, a few of them doing so with great enjoyment.

Adolf Hitler laughed uproariously in private conversations as he talked about the mass murder of the Jews of Europe that he had unleashed.

At the very same moment, thousands of Europeans like Oskar Schindler were risking their lives to give shelter, food, and care to the hunted Jews themselves.

Tonight, in many homes on many continents, mothers and fathers will tenderly sing their little children to sleep, covering their tiny faces with kisses as they tuck them into bed.

Tonight, in many homes on many continents, mothers and fathers and boyfriends and strangers will molest, torment, and beat little children, who (if they survive the night) will cry themselves to sleep, covering their tiny faces with tears as they lay in their beds.

When my children were young enough to watch *Sesame Street,* a refrain often wafted through our house:"One of these things is not like the other; one of these things just doesn't belong." Child abuse and infinite parental tenderness; genocide and rescue; abolitionism and sadistic slaveholding; mercy ministry and cannibalism—one of these things is not like the other; one of these things just doesn't belong. Both exist, however. Both are expressions of human nature. Both are recurring human possibilities.

Both Jeffrey Dahmer and Mother Teresa undoubtedly enjoyed a warm blanket on a cold night, relief from pain, a laugh with a friend, shelter from the elements. They shared the basic needs that all human beings share. Yet when we contemplate the breathtaking differences between their actions or between the actions of Hitler and Schindler, we remain compelled to ask this question: Is there really a shared "human nature" to be found here? Are such divergent individuals widely varying examples of the same species, or are they so different that any effort to describe them as "alike" is an artificial imposition that overrides the real evidence before us? What exactly *is* this human nature that is supposed to exist? How can we talk about life's journey in any general sense if the human beings who undertake such journeys are so very different from each other?

This extraordinary plasticity in human nature, this wide variation in the character and actions of creatures supposedly sharing the same nature, is surely perplexing, but historic Christian belief has never wavered in its claim that a common, shared human nature actually exists. Christians have differed in how they describe certain aspects of human nature but not in their basic belief that there is something there to describe.

As we revisit what Christians have believed about the most perplexing questions related to human nature, we'll see that these beliefs are contested by competing secular and religious visions of human nature. We will gain a fuller sense of why this subject is so vital, not just to the Christian experience of life's journey, but also to our collective journey in a broader society and in the world.

> *Christians have differed in how they describe certain aspects of human nature but not in their basic belief that there is something there to describe.*

But we cannot offer any meaningful presentation of what Christians have believed about human nature without first dealing with the claim some make today that there is no such thing as human nature at all. If we cannot answer yes to the question of whether human nature exists, we will have a hard time answering the questions posed in other chapters. So this is where we must begin—with the question of whether such a thing as human nature exists at all or whether each human being stands unique and alone in undertaking the journey of life.

SOMETHING'S THERE: HISTORIC CHRISTIAN BELIEF

To understand historic Christian (and Jewish) thought and belief, all roads lead back to the first chapters of Genesis, even its first words:"In the beginning God created the heavens and the earth" (Genesis 1:1). Reading Genesis presents no small challenge, because the question of how these first chapters are best interpreted has bedeviled scholars for centuries, especially since the rise of modern science. But few things are more depressing and fruitless than arguments pitting creationists against evolutionists, especially as they debate Genesis 1 and 2. No, the point of the opening section of the Bible is its depiction of God—and of all that God has created, including human beings. There is a beauty to these majestic words about our origins that are intended to spark our sense of wonder at the majesty and mystery of creation. As the American rabbi Solomon Goldman put it, Genesis "is Jewish genius brooding on God. It is the progenitors of the Jewish people examining and discarding the views of Creator and creation universally held in their day. . . . Its God is transcendent and yet so human; its man so earthly and yet so godlike. Its appeal is universal and yet reads as if it were intended for us alone. Its air is familiar and yet an immortal freshness rests upon it."[1]

As we enter this majestic story, we find that on the sixth day of creation, after an orderly world luxuriant with life has been created, human beings first make their appearance in the Bible as an idea in the mind of God—an idea that he tries out on whoever is listening to his deliberations: "Let us make humankind in our image, according to our likeness" (Genesis 1:26). And God proceeds to do just that: "So God created humankind in his image, in the image of God he created them, male and female he created them" (1:28).

In Genesis 2:4–25, the creation of humanity is depicted as a two-step process involving God's "hands-on" activity. In this account, God stoops down to form man from the "dust of the ground" and then breathes life into him, at which point he "became a living being" (2:7). Later God forms the woman from the very substance of the man (2:22–23). The two then stand before God as the first human beings. They immediately join their lives together in unashamed union.

Either account, but especially the first, carries within it the core biblical conviction that *God designed and created human beings in an initial dramatic act as bearers of a special and distinctive nature.* From these first pages until its very end, the Bible speaks of human beings in ways that are consistent with this account of our divine origins. The story is that the God of the universe is our Maker. He has given all human beings who have ever lived a nature that has been transmitted to us through those first two people and all who have come after them. We are creatures of a certain type, and that type was established by our Designer from the beginning. This belief came forward through the centuries, with the Israelites, to the Jews and then to those followers of Jesus who came to be known as Christians.

The story takes a dark turn, however. That original human nature was not to remain as God designed it. From the first, we have also seemed prone to temptation and sin, as the famous story of the first sin reminds us (Genesis 3). The narrative may seem fanciful: a talking serpent tempts the first woman to eat a forbidden fruit, she and her husband both eat it, and the red flashing sirens enter human history, never to leave again. Take the story as poetry or take it as history, as you will; however you take it, only the most naïve or the willfully blind can deny the reality of sin that it so powerfully describes—temptation, dishonesty, disobedience, rebellion, deception, evasion, conviction, and punishment. The human condition indeed!

There are many momentous questions that could be asked about this mysterious, stubborn, and terrible dimension of human life. Did God create us with an intentional or unintentional "design flaw" that makes us susceptible to sin? If we started off perfect, and God is perfect in his knowledge of everything, including his own creatures, how could he have made creatures that would mess up as badly as we do? Are we left with the alternative that God intended for us to descend into sin to test us, to make us dependent on him or so that he could then rescue us? Is sin a necessary aspect of life's journey? Or do we need to abandon the basic biblical framework and reject the idea of an original sinless state soon corrupted by sin? Are there perhaps other ways of interpreting the significance of this primeval story?

Because I will devote an entire chapter to the issue of sin later in the book, and it will never be far from our view as the central hazard on life's journey, we will defer further consideration until later. For now, what matters is the biblical teaching that the decision of Adam and Eve to deliberately disobey God affected not just themselves but every one of us thereafter. In fact, the Apostle Paul says that the *entire created order* is "groaning in labor pains" and in "bondage to decay" as a result of human sin (Romans 8:21–22). Just as we human beings were all included in Adam's glorious creation, we are just as much all included in his catastrophic rebellion and consequent punishment (5:12–14). The upshot here is the Christian belief that a shared human nature exists in *creation*, because all humans are made in the image of God; in *sin*, because "all have sinned and fall short of the glory of God" (3:23); in standing under *divine judgment*, because due to sin, "no human being will be justified in his sight" (3:20); and in the possibility of *redemption*, because "God so loved the world that he gave his only Son, so that everyone who believes in him may not perish but have eternal life" (John 3:16). The entire biblical framework of thought assumes a collective, shared human nature rooted in a collective, shared human journey from creation through sin to redemption made possible in Jesus Christ. Every human being who is born enters that shared human journey and crafts his or her own journey within that context.

This means that in Christian thought, we are left with the unshakable conviction that a Jeffrey Dahmer and a Mother Teresa are in fact both human beings created according to God's design, stained by sin, and objects of God's redemptive love in Jesus Christ. They are both human beings, inescapably bound to a shared identity that transcends the different paths they took with their lives. Perhaps if we join our journey

> *The entire biblical framework of thought assumes a collective, shared human nature rooted in a collective, shared human journey from creation through sin to redemption made possible in Jesus Christ.*

image to a mountaineering image, we can say that people like Teresa and Wilberforce rise to the heights of what is possible in human nature, whereas murderers like Dahmer and Hitler illustrate how deep our descent into sin can go. But both kinds of people are still people. And both kinds of journeys can be understood within the framework of the biblical world of thought.

MADE IN THE IMAGE OF GOD

In the Christian tradition, then, human nature exists, it is marked by enduring evidence of divine design as well as human sin, and its essentials are shared among all human beings. There is another important dimension of this set of core biblical convictions that must be teased out. This is the pivotal claim in Genesis that all humans are made in the image of God. The same claim is actually made three times in the first nine chapters of the Bible (Genesis 1:28, 5:1–2, 9:6). Despite its familiarity, it is a phrase that is enigmatic to us because there is little in our contemporary experience with similar implications. What does it mean to say that we are made in the *imago dei,* the image of God?

The phrase carries a rich range of meanings, but we will focus on just two of them. In one sense it expresses a unique human *resemblance* to God, not physically (for God is spirit and has no body), but spiritually. To be made in God's image means something like the idea that one can look in the mirror as a human being and see traces of the divine being who designed us. We resemble God in our capacity to love, to reason, to feel, to relate to other creatures, to imagine, to plan, to create, to contemplate, and in many other ways. We are an image of God—a scratched-up one, badly damaged by sin, but the evidence of God's nature and character is in us, especially when we ascend to our highest potential. As the British theologian Alister McGrath put it, "Within each of us exists the image of God, however disfigured and corrupted by sin it may presently be."[2]

Another key aspect of the image of God has to do with a unique human *responsibility* before God and in relation to all other creatures. This has historically been called the "dominion mandate," based on Genesis 1:26: "And let them have dominion over the fish of the sea, and over the birds of the air, and over the cattle, and over all the wild animals of the earth. . . ." This concept has been easily misunderstood to mean mastery, domination, and exploitation; indeed, some (both advocates and critics) think it cannot be understood in any other way. But a clue from the context in which Genesis was written helps us do much

> *To be made in God's image means something like the idea that one can look in the mirror as a human being and see traces of the divine being who designed us.*

better here. In the ancient Near Eastern world in which the book of Genesis was written, kings would sometimes want to signal their sovereignty over an area without going to the spot themselves. They would therefore send representatives, who carried with them flags or other insignia bearing the image of the king. The message was, "I can't be here myself, but this image and the one who bears it represent me." This is what Genesis means by the phrase "image of God." It is as if God is saying to us, "I choose you to represent me to this planet and all its inhabitants. You are in charge. You act in my

name, bearing my image. You are responsible to represent me
well." This deeply enriches our understanding of the *imago
dei*. It lifts up the unique and extraordinary responsibility that
human beings have in relation to all of this world's creatures
and the planet itself. But if we understand God rightly, especially through the lens of Jesus Christ, we will see that to represent a God like the God we meet in Christ is to serve, not
to dominate. "For [Jesus] came not to be served but to serve,
and to give his life a ransom for many" (Matthew 20:28).

Whether we emphasize divine resemblance or divinely
given responsibility, the concept of the *imago dei* has tremen-
dous implications for our understanding of human nature.
Take, for example, the idea of human equality. To say that
humankind is made in the image of God is to say that *all* human beings, none excepted, share this character and status,
regardless of where they start off in life or what they make of
life's journey. This creates critically important moral obligations
for each one of us. If all human beings are made in the image
of God, they must be viewed as such—collectively and indi-
vidually—and likewise must be treated with appropriate dignity (even Dahmer, even Hitler). Each specific human being I
encounter is made in the image of God. Whoever she is, whatever her condition, status, or character, she must be treated
with the dignity of one made in God's image. As she pursues
her life's journey, she has worth fully equivalent to mine.

Likewise, the Bible itself demands that violations of the
image of God (that is, violations of human beings made in
the divine image) be punished. "Whoever sheds the blood of
a human, by a human shall that person's blood be shed; for
in his own image God made humankind" (Genesis 9:6). To
murder a person is to strike at the image of God, and this
must be deterred, prevented, and punished if necessary

(Romans 13:1–7). There is a kind of sacredness associated with human life, a zone of reverence, which must be guarded and honored. It applies to all human beings, without exceptions, because all are made in the image of God.

The implications of *imago dei* have been pivotal for several millennia in undercutting hierarchical, stratified, and racist beliefs of all types and in encouraging mercy and justice for all. Certainly, these norms have often been honored more in the breach than in reality, but those in the biblical tradition have regularly found themselves returning to this wellspring of moral renewal and reform—in the fights against slavery, child labor, forced prostitution, war, genocide, torture, infanticide, totalitarianism, and many other battles. For the concept of the image of God, embedded in the canon and the tradition, stands in judgment of our sins when we violate it. One of those sins is to draw any kind of fundamental distinction between types, groups, or sections of human beings. Whatever very real differences do exist between various individuals and various groups of people, the conviction that all are made in the image of God provides a nonnegotiable basis for belief in a shared nature that dictates how all are to be treated.

Associated with the concept of *imago dei* in biblical thought has been the conviction that its attribution to human beings *alone* in the biblical story sets humankind apart from all other creatures, elevating us to a higher status before God. This is not to say that the rest of the created order, from plants to animals to the very earth and air themselves, have no value before God. Quite the contrary: the creation account depicts their divine origination in loving detail. All of creation has value because it was all dreamed up in the mind of God and created at his command. All creatures are declared "good" as they are created (see Genesis 1:23, 25), and the Bible depicts God's independent relationship with all creatures (consider Psalm 104). They are included in the covenant that God makes with the entire created order through Noah after the flood (Genesis 9:10ff.). The animals exhibit a composite body-soul identity that marks them as remarkably similar to human beings (for more on this, see Chapter Two). Like us, they live as long as the blood circulates and the "breath of life" (Genesis 2:7) flows through them, and they die when these miracles cease. As the moral thinker and theologian Larry Rasmussen has pointed out, human beings share this planet as an "earth community" with all other creatures.[3]

And yet, despite the sacredness of all creation, only human beings are described as being made in the image of God, as being "a little lower than God" in status, as "crowned with glory and honor" (Psalm 8:5). We have a spiritual nature and capacity that even the highest animals have not been granted. We are depicted as responsible for exercising stewardship and providing leadership over all creatures of the planet, rather than the other way around (Genesis 1:28–31; Psalm 8:6–8). Thus one aspect of the historic Christian concept of a real human nature is found right here, in the clear distinction drawn between human beings and other creatures—despite our shared status as creatures and shared location as inhabitants of earth—as well as the higher responsibility that human beings are granted in relation to the other creatures.

The concept of the image of God also points to a related conviction about human nature. That is the biblically rooted belief that human nature is fixed or static, at least in its essentials. This most emphatically does not mean that people never change or that cultures do not differ dramatically from one another. But even acknowledging these great variations, Christians have believed that it is possible to speak of an essence of "man" or "humanity" as a more or less given, fixed, unchanging, and unchangeable reality across all cultures, all nations, and all eras. Fundamentally, this is rooted in the basic sweep of the biblical story running from creation through the fall of humanity, its many trials, and finally to redemption in Jesus Christ.

This vision of a shared human nature that persists across time and culture allows us to examine the elements of that nature in more detail. The Christian ethicist Sondra Wheeler offers one standard list from within our faith tradition when she says that human beings are *created* (we come from God and do not make ourselves), *embodied* (we have bodies), *social* (we live in community), *sinful* (we do wrong and choose bad over good), *mortal* (we die), and *redeemed* (we are the recipients of God's grace, his forgiving love).[4] From a scientific perspective rooted in observations of human cultures, the anthropologist Donald E. Brown has compiled a list of hundreds of "human universals," which he argues are shared across all cultures; these range from abstract thought to classification of kin to inheritance rules.[5] It is really quite a staggering and lengthy list.

So a variety of things could be said, and have been said, about this essentially given, fixed, shared human nature. But one can't say anything about "man" or "humanity" or "the human person" or the "human condition" without first assuming that there is something there to talk about, some common attributes that remain constant in all circumstances. Certainly the more careful Christian thinkers have recognized that human beings make diverse choices and live in vastly different circumstances, and so their lives are open to various paths. But the tradition has always affirmed that these paths are charted within certain boundaries set by human nature itself, a nature with a basic structure that is inescapable and unalterable. As the eighteenth-century social observer Lady Mary Wortley Montagu wrote, "I have never, in all my various travels, seen but two sorts of people. . . . I mean men and women, who always have been, and ever will be, the same. The same vices and the same follies have been the fruit of all ages, though sometimes under different names."[6]

CHALLENGES TO *IMAGO DEI*

It is no surprise that this Christian understanding of human nature is not the only explanation for who we are and why we are that way. Over the past several centuries, a number of challenges have arisen to compete with the Christian view of human nature. Some of these have merely been quibbles with one or another dimension of Christian belief. The most far-reaching have raised questions about whether there is such a thing as human nature at all or if there is whether the historic biblical tradition offers a truthful account of it.

Readers who are happy to trust what they understand to be the treatment of human nature offered by the Bible or Christian tradition might wonder why they should care about the challenges offered by various unorthodox thinkers or contending schools of thought. To this I would respond that burying our heads in the sand is rarely an adequate response to life's challenges, be they intellectual or otherwise. Christian faith is on the retreat across wide swaths of the Western world, and one reason for this retreat is our regular unwillingness or inability to confront the most searching questions that are being posed in our world today.

Engaging our critics, rather than ignoring them, also gives us the opportunity to deepen and refine our understanding of our own tradition and beliefs. We may find that we can incorporate our critics' legitimate points into our beliefs while jettisoning whatever does not stand up to scrutiny. Or we may discover allies in unexpected places, people who do not necessarily share all our beliefs but who offer key insights or support for some of our most cherished convictions. Of course, there are certain criticisms of the Christian concept of human nature that cannot be incorporated in any way because they represent a fundamental clash of worldviews, featuring beliefs that are simply irreconcilable. Engaging those critics helps us identify our truly nonnegotiable beliefs.

HUMAN NATURE OR MALE NATURE?

As we consider major challenges to the idea that such a thing as human nature exists, let's start off with the *feminist* critique that what the Western (Christian) tradition takes as *human* nature has actually been a rendering of *male* nature that has left half the species invisible and unaccounted for.

Feminist thinkers such as Rosemary Ruether and Mary Daly, and many in earlier generations such as Elizabeth Cady Stanton and Frances Willard, have noticed the undeniable fact that the biblical traditions (both Judaism and Christianity, not to mention the postbiblical Islamic tradition) have been male-dominated faiths. The central figures of the traditions themselves have been male (Abraham, Isaac, Jacob, Moses, Jesus, Peter, Paul). God has been addressed with male pronouns and depicted in art and custom as a male figure. Scripture was written by men and geared to men, though this is true of some passages more than others. Men dominate religious leadership in the Bible. The theological traditions through the ages have been primarily interpreted by men, from the "church fathers" till today. And it is not at all difficult to find numerous statements denigrating women from some of the leading Jewish, Christian, and Islamic religious thinkers, perhaps summed up most succinctly by the first-century Jewish writer Josephus when he wrote, "A woman is inferior to man in every way."[7]

The feminist movement that swept the Western world, especially its second wave beginning in the 1960s, has long been engaged in a thoroughgoing reevaluation of both Judaism and Christianity that began with the simple recognition that these faith traditions have been dominated by men. Some feminist thinkers work from within the biblical traditions to balance the scales a bit—to take account of the women who appear in the Bible, who have provided religious leadership, and who are doing important work today. More radical feminists are convinced that the Western religious traditions are not retrievable for women, drenched as they are in male domination.

It is in the context of this highly significant rethinking of biblical faith that feminist challenges to the concept of human nature have been offered. The observation that men have dominated the Christian tradition, for example, elicits the natural question of whether the account offered of human nature in that tradition has been distorted by accounting only for the male experience. What if traditional theology has actually offered an account of *male* nature rather than *human* (meaning men's and women's) nature?

Of course, the answer to this question presupposes the belief that male and female natures actually differ in some fundamental ways. This is one of the most contested issues in feminist thought, not to mention in the broader culture. Is there a single human nature, which both men and women share? (If so, why do we have so much difficulty understanding and relating to each other?) Are there radically distinct male and female natures, with little or no overlap? (If so, how can we be a single species, made in God's image?) Or is it a "both/and" situation, as I think that both Scripture and experience suggest, in which there is a core of shared human characteristics along with others that are distinctively male and female, with cultural patterns affecting both shared and distinctive characteristics?

The basic Christian account of human nature that I have offered so far is general enough to accommodate feminist objections, at least those that do not abandon belief in some core *human* nature that both male and female share. When we say that human nature exists and is given by God, that all are made in God's image, that all are affected by sin, and that in its essential features human nature changes little, those claims apply equally well to male and female. But when we get into more detailed thinking about human responsibility, sinfulness, freedom, community, and other issues, we must be mindful of the concern that feminist voices raise, or we will indeed be at risk of fundamental misunderstandings of human nature as *both* males and females experience it. For example, most presentations of the problem of human sin emphasize pride—thinking too highly of oneself, making oneself the center of the universe. But they don't talk as much about self-hatred, or thinking too poorly of oneself. Women who write about sin remind us that more women are likely to struggle with self-loathing than with arrogance. Listening to women's voices on issues like this helps us avoid an account of human nature that simply becomes an account of male nature.

LICENSE TO EXPLOIT EARTH
AND ITS CREATURES?

A second critique of the classic Christian concept of human nature might be called the *ecological–animal rights* perspective. This actually began as two separate critiques, but their concerns have converged sufficiently to consider them together here.

Ever since 1967, when the historian Lynn White Jr., claimed in a famous *Science* magazine article that biblical theology was ultimately responsible for the ecological crisis, Christians (and Jews) have found themselves facing significant challenges to their understanding of human nature from the environmental movement.[8]

In terms of Scripture itself, the challenge is directed, first, against the exalted status of humans in relation to the rest of the earth's creatures and, second, against the so-called dominion mandate given to human beings. In attempting to sort through how Western civilization had come to treat the earth with such reckless disregard, some thinkers like White traced the roots of the problem back to these central biblical texts. Only a civilization—so it was claimed—whose holy book taught human beings to set themselves above and in dominion over other creatures and to see the world not as sacred but as a natural resource to be exploited could have produced the kind of environmental problems that beset us.

Of course, many Christians dismissed such claims out of hand. They pointed to what they saw as the real culprits: recent historical developments, such as the rise of capitalism and industrialism, of science and modern technology, and even the decline of Christianity in the Western world in favor of rationalism and empiricism.

Thoughtful, less defensive Christians have in recent years tried to take White's critique to heart through a fresh rereading of the Bible. While some Christian thinkers have responded to environmentalist critics by abandoning historic Christian claims to a unique status for human beings or to any kind of human sovereignty over the earth, more moderate voices have found the answer in Scripture itself. I count myself among those who have been rightly appalled by the degradation that human beings have visited upon the planet as well as our atrocious mistreatment of animals. But I believe that the Bible itself, rightly interpreted, offers a vision of human beings living in harmony with the created order and exercising responsible managerial stewardship over the earth and its creatures. The reality of our extraordinary scientific and technological powers and their great impact on the earth now clearly show that we have no choice but to exercise the *right kind* of leadership and "dominion." There is no going back to a preindustrial paradise. Either we human beings learn to live in sustainable community with the earth and other creatures, or we are all doomed.

There is also no reason to be found within the Bible itself to deny the many commonalities between human beings and animals or to lose a sense of wonder and reverence for all living things, including animals. Our unique status as human beings need not be read as a license

> *I believe that the Bible itself offers a vision of human beings living in harmony with the created order and exercising responsible managerial stewardship over the earth and its creatures.*

to dominate but instead a mandate to serve, just as Jesus' unique status among us was for him a mandate to serve, as he illustrated when he washed his disciples' feet at the Last Supper (John 13:1–20; compare Philippians 2:1–11). Christians who would maintain fidelity to the biblical witness cannot give up the claim that human beings have a unique status before God, but we must just as surely rediscover the full community of creatures with whom we share this planet and to whom we have God-given responsibilities. As the Christian philosopher Robert Wennberg has written, this actually entails the need for a dramatic reformation of our treatment of animals ·especially in "factory farming" and medical research.[9]

NO GOD, NO GOD-GIVEN HUMAN NATURE?

Perhaps the most fundamental objection to the Christian belief in a God-given human nature is the claim that it is a convenient myth invented by insecure creatures whose existence on this planet is best explained as a kind of cosmic accident and who cannot bear to face the facts. There is no God—or no personal God or no God who interacts with human beings. We were not planted here by any omnipotent designer but emerged on earth through an evolutionary process whose beginnings are shrouded in chance and mystery. Out of a cosmic soup of raw materials, human beings (and other creatures) emerged as a kind of accident. Perhaps unfortunately for us, we were the creatures who also developed an intelligence and self-consciousness that made it necessary for us to try to find explanations for our existence and an order to the cosmos. We have been trying to do this through all recorded history, but all such explanations (at least all such explanations involving a supernatural component) are mythological.

This perspective, often called the *naturalist* or *materialist* view (the belief that the only reality is the material world and that there is no supernatural reality or beings associated with it), obviously leads to the abandonment of a belief in human nature as a purposefully designed set of characteristics imprinted on us by a divine being. We were not designed or made or created by anybody. We just happened and developed into the kinds of creatures we now are over an incomprehensibly long period of time.

> *Although it is possible to hold to an evolutionary perspective that does not negate Christian beliefs about human nature, the most commonly articulated view of evolution today represents a frontal assault on such convictions.*

This evolutionary perspective, closely associated with the materialist view, presents significant challenges to the classic Christian belief about human nature. Although it is possible to hold to an evolutionary perspective that does not negate Christian beliefs about human nature, the most commonly articulated view of evolution today represents a frontal assault on such convictions.

Evolutionary theorists believe that what we now know as human beings emerged slowly from the animal kingdom over many millennia, constantly evolving in response to challenges presented by the world around them until they became the species we now call *Homo sapiens*. Contrary to the classical Christian account, human beings were not created in a single dramatic act with a set of characteristics that remains largely the same today as a millennia ago. To the contrary, human beings and what we understand to be human nature are dynamic, always changing in response to various natural and historic challenges and realities. We are a species that does not stand still but in fact changes constantly, and our capacity for change has been crucial to our existence, survival, and flourishing.

Full-blown evolutionary perspectives on human nature abandon reference to historic religious or moral beliefs, explaining all phenomena of human experience in evolutionary terms. For example, it abandons the idea that sin is violation of God's will, a will revealed in Scripture and written on the human heart, and that its origins are found in the temptation to mistrust and disobey God. Instead, scholars offer explanations that trace conflicting human drives and the uneasy feelings they produce back to adaptation, natural selection, and other elements of our long evolutionary pilgrimage. In a typical expression of this perspective, the Harvard University cognitive science researcher Steven Pinker says, "Like all living things, we are outcomes of natural selection; we got here because we inherited traits that allowed our ancestors to survive, find mates, and reproduce. This momentous fact explains our deepest strivings."[10] An entire cottage industry has emerged over the past several decades offering evolutionary ("sociobiological") explanations for human nature in its various aspects. Sociobiology seems to have superseded psychoanalytic theory as the major contemporary competitor to the Christian account of human behavior.

If one reads a bit in secular literature about human nature, it does not take long to see the bitter argument between those who now reject the very existence of a human nature and others who do not. The "blank slate" view, which emerged especially from the social sciences during the mid-twentieth century but is still easily found today, is the idea that humans have no nature but that each of us is *entirely conditioned* by culture, environment, and experience—in other words, *we are our journey, nothing more.* Thus the comment in 1935 from the Spanish philosopher and revolutionary Jose Ortega y Gasset that opened the chapter: "Man has no nature; what he has is history."[11] Each of us is what we have experienced, and no more.

The blank-slate perspective correlates well with the belief that human nature is the opposite of shared, given, fixed, or static but is instead infinitely variable, plastic, dynamic, and individual. The British playwright and writer Oscar Wilde put it well when he wrote, "The only thing that one really knows about human nature is that it changes. . . . The systems that fail are those that rely on the permanency of human nature, and not on its growth and development."[12] Such a view, now widely shared, highlights human freedom, human changeability, and the inescapable necessity to direct one's own life journey. It would be fair to say that this perspective sees not human *being* but only individual, diverse, and irreducibly unique human *beings,* the products of their own choices (and, alas, the choices of others) but not representatives of a consistent type of creature with predictable characteristics.

Steven Pinker, quoted earlier, is among those who have joined the argument vigorously from the other side. Pinker is most insistent that there is indeed a human nature and that the best contemporary science clearly demonstrates it. Working with the study of the brain (cognitive neuroscience), genetics, evolutionary psychology, and anthropology, Pinker becomes a kind of surprising ally to Christian convictions in offering a very strong argument for the existence of a human nature that is universally shared. Pinker does not in any way deny the fact that individuals and cultures vary dramatically in how they build on, express, and develop their innate capacities. But at the base of all of these possible developments is a kind of "programming" that we all share.[13] Thus he explains both the commonalities and the diversities in human nature by claiming that we share an inborn "programming," which we each then put to work in diverse ways to generate an "unlimited set of thoughts and behavior."[14]

Before we draw too much comfort from Pinker, it is important to note that he explicitly rejects the Christian account of human nature. He rejects the concept of a soul or self in favor of an explanation for human consciousness drawn from cognitive neuroscience. And he embraces the evolutionary perspective as "central to the understanding of life, including human life."[15]

There is little in the materialistic-evolutionary view of human beings that can be helpfully incorporated into a Christian perspective that keeps faith with biblical claims. We cannot accept a naturalistic reading of reality or of the origins of human life. While some of us are open to accepting that humans have been on a long evolutionary pilgrimage that has brought us many changes, we are not able or willing to abandon belief that God is our Creator, that human nature has a divine design, or that the concepts of sin and redemption are meaningful. We cannot accept the belief that there is no human nature but instead only infinite diversity and the nausea of choice without boundaries, choice without direction. Nor can we accept a concept of human nature stripped, as Pinker has done, of its selfhood, soul, conscience, and relationship with a Creator who is its ultimate origin and destiny.

There is yet one more challenge to a Christian account of human nature, with implications that cast a shadow over the future of humanity, other creatures, and the planet itself. Developments in genetics, transgenics (interspecies genetic mixing), artificial intelligence, cybernetics (the blending and integration of technology and humanity), and nanotechnology (engineering on the molecular and subatomic level) are bringing numerous unprecedented possibilities into view. Human beings have, or will soon have, the ability to remake their own bodies in innumerable ways, to custom-design their children, to replace dead loved ones with clones, to mix themselves with animals or machines, to integrate technology into the human brain or other parts of the body, or to create any kind of hybrid animal that we want. While some of us, especially people of faith, react to such developments with caution, many voices can be heard saying that this is just the next stage in human evolution, as in this statement from the World Transhumanist Association: "Humanity will be radically changed by technology in the future. We foresee the feasibility of redesigning the human condition, including such parameters as the inevitability of aging, limitations on human and artificial intellects, unchosen psychology, suffering, and our confinement to the planet Earth."[16]

If human life is a cosmic accident and our current nature (if it exists) is merely where we happen to be in the evolutionary process right now, and if we can imagine ways to remake ourselves (or other organic or inorganic creatures) that would be more "adaptive" for the human future, and if we are free to do whatever we want to do, why not proceed? Why not create a *posthuman* or *transhuman* future and leave this pitiful creature *Homo sapiens* behind in favor of a better model? As C. S. Lewis memorably put it, "*Human* nature will be the last part of Nature to surrender to Man."[17] It may be that only those who hold on to an understanding of human nature whose roots extend much farther back into human history than current views will provide the wisdom we need to keep us from collectively proceeding on a journey that may remake humanity beyond recognition or even, in a worst-case scenario, destroy humanity altogether.

It's a sobering prospect, but I believe that the Christian perspective offers our best respite, our best means for judging the options proliferating before us. Clearly, the belief in a God who created us and the rest of this world leads us toward a different sense of what it means for humans to grow toward wholeness. In the next chapter, we will look inside the human self, see what mysteries we might be able to find there, and reflect on what the makeup of the human self tells us about the journey of human life.

What Am I Made Of?

Man is a little soul carrying around a corpse.
—MARCUS AURELIUS, SECOND-CENTURY
ROMAN EMPEROR AND PHILOSOPHER

One of the most amazing facts about human beings is that all six billion of us walk around in our own skin all day long, a single species created by God, and yet we have never been able to agree on how to think about what we are made of, what our constituent parts look like, *what we are.*

Think about yourself for just a minute. Look at your arms and legs, your hands and feet, maybe even your fingers and toes. Listen to yourself internally as you read the words on this page. Feel the activity in your brain as you process the words you are reading and the thoughts these words are evoking. Read about your reading. Think about your thinking.

Now answer these questions: Are you a body, or do you *have* a body? If you have a body but are not a body, what else are you? Are you perhaps a "soul" and a body? Is the "you"— or the "real" you—centered in the soul? What then is the status of your body? What is the connection between the soul and the body that you have or are?

Or perhaps the language of spirit makes more sense to you. Are you a spirit? Or are you a *person* who has both a body and a spirit? What of the soul then? Perhaps you are a person consisting of body, soul, and spirit? What then would be the distinctions between soul and spirit? What would be the connections among all three elements?

Maybe you are *now* a human being who has both a body and a spirit or a body and a spirit and a soul. Were you always that? What were you before you were born? Anything? What will you be after you die? Anything? Are you now a person with body and soul but before you were born and after you die you were and will again be a soul without a body? What would that kind of existence be like?

There are few answers to these mindbending questions that everyone agrees on, even the people who have thought most deeply about them. We are confused about issues that can hardly be more fundamental to what it means to be human. Think about it: *we don't even know what we are.* Isn't that amazing? Perhaps we will never be able to do more than speculate about what we are or what we are made of. But we must ask about such things if we want to understand human nature. And in the quest for wholeness, it is hard to imagine finding it if we do not unify the inner regions of the self.

WHAT'S INSIDE US?

As a starting point, let's assume that we know that we have a body. Although some philosophers were not even sure about that, even so we can guess that they probably ate dinner most nights, went to the bathroom, and closed their eyes to sleep. If some people want to debate whether they have a body, we will leave them to it, but we will assume that, yes, we know that we have a body. We feed it, bathe it, rest it, exercise it, and use it in a variety of other ways. We know that when we die, this body will cease to function. It will lie still, inert. It will begin to decay, so our friends and family will have to bury or destroy it.

But few of us are willing to believe that we are only a body. For one thing, we have thoughts, sometimes very searching (and sometimes very superficial) ones. These thoughts are centered in what we have historically thought of as our mind. We now know that the activity we identify as the work of the mind is located in the brain. Some people think that the work of the mind is simply activity of the brain. Extremely sophisticated scientific research has specified what kind of mental functioning happens in particular regions of the brain. But even so, most of us stubbornly persist in believing that there is more to us than nerve impulses and firing synapses, that we are more than wondrously sophisticated neurological supercomputers. There is something else there—our souls, our spirits, *something*. Isn't there?

In this chapter, I cannot promise an account of "what we are made of" that will satisfy all seekers. It's not easy to overcome deep divisions in understandings of the human self. Instead, we'll explore the main competing approaches to describing the different parts of a human being, including a Christian perspective

> *Most of us stubbornly persist in believing that there is more to us than nerve impulses and firing synapses, that we are more than wondrously sophisticated neurological supercomputers.*

that I think makes the best sense of both what the Bible says and what we experience when we look deeply inside ourselves to find out what is in there.

BODY AND SOUL

Perhaps the most commonly held belief in our culture about what we are made of is that each of us is a two-part entity containing body and soul. The body is the physical structure and material substance of the human being, while the soul is the interior spiritual part of a person. How these two parts coexist in one person has been imagined and described in varying ways. The simplest depiction has divided the self into two parts or substances, as shown most simply in Figure 2.1. The subtle implication of this crude line drawing is that though we are made up of two quite different constituent parts, both are necessary, both are equal in value, and both are fundamental to what it means to be human.

But in the history of Western and sometimes Christian thought, this has not been the primary way of describing the relationship between body and soul. Beginning with Plato, the body was quite often viewed as inferior and subordinate to the soul, as less real and less valuable, even as a prison for

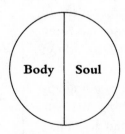

Figure 2.1

the soul. An anonymous quote makes the point quite strikingly: "The body is just a shell for the real person."[1] Or in the words of the Roman emperor and philosopher Marcus Aurelius, quoted at the beginning of the chapter, "Man is a little soul carrying around a corpse."

In this view, the true self is the soul. It is housed in the body, because at least on this planet and in this species, souls do not roam free but must be embodied somewhere. The implication is that the soul could do just as well—indeed, far better—if freed from the constraints and difficulties of the body and allowed to enjoy an unfettered spiritual existence. This appears to be what the Apostle Paul is saying in 2 Corinthians 5 when he writes, apparently in a moment of great distress, "For in this [bodily] tent we groan, longing to be clothed with our heavenly dwelling. . . . We would rather be away from the body and at home with the Lord" (2 Corinthians 5:2, 8).

This view has tended to reflect and reinforce a vision of reality in which, almost by definition, what is visible is less real and less valuable than what is invisible. Our experience of life within our bodies and their five senses are real enough until some philosopher, preacher, or theologian teaches us to believe that what is invisible within people, between people, and in the supernatural realm is what is most real and most valuable. In the end, this view can train us not to see the material world with much clarity or to care about it with much intensity because we are so busy training our eyes on what we cannot see. The heaven we cannot see becomes more real than the suffering neighbor that we can see if we would just open our eyes and look.

One deeply ingrained reason for this elevation of the value of the (invisible) soul over the (visible) body has been a depreciation of the body itself. The body has been disparaged for all kinds of reasons, both for its own properties and characteristics (real or imagined) and by comparison with the properties and characteristics of the soul (real or imagined).

For one thing, the body constantly changes. The developmental process of the human body from conception to birth to death consists of a never-ending sequence of changes. The body never stays still, a fact long observed but never more clearly than through contemporary scientific discoveries related to such things as fetal development and the nature of the brain. For people who are disturbed by change, who view change as inferior to unchangeableness, such as most of the Greek philosophical tradition, this makes the body a questionable entity indeed. The soul, by contrast, has often been viewed as unchanging, not just through the human life span but both before birth and after death.

Likewise, the body suffers. It is susceptible to pain under slight variations of desired conditions—it hungers, thirsts, feels cold, feels hot, gets sick in an endless variety of ways, and so on. This propensity to suffer from bodily needs has been contrasted with the soul's freedom from such urges and needs. How we yearn to be free of all our physical suffering! Just as I was completing this book, I accidentally plunged a kitchen knife into the area between my thumb and index finger on my right hand. Stupid accident; extreme physical pain. I fainted and threw up; for forty-five minutes, I barely knew where I was. All other capacities that I had completely gave way to the struggle to regain my equilibrium and get relief from my pain. No wonder people have preferred a soul that feels no pain.

The body also gets dirty, emits foul smells, excretes. A primal disgust at the humble physical functions of the human body and their inescapable carnality and earthiness has often led thinkers and philosophers to disparage the body in favor of a soul viewed as clean, pure, and unsullied by the body's dirt and grime.

The body has sex. Not only does it participate in sex, but it seems to be the center of desire for sex. The sexually hungry person can often feel the desire for sexual release right in the body itself, as a kind of tingling ache. Certainly this hunger for sex, and the raw "animal" passion of sex, has sometimes been the primary source of disdain for the body, in contrast to the supposedly sexless soul. The fourth-century church father Lactantius said, "Those who indulge in pleasure and give way to lust hand their souls over to their body and condemn it to death; inasmuch as they make themselves their body's slaves, and over the body death has power."[2]

Lactantius is not just saying that lust is a victory of the body over the soul, which is bad, but that *the reason this is bad is that the body dies.* Anything that dies is inferior to something that does not die. This is perhaps the primary reason why the body has been deemed less worthy than the soul. As the Apostle James says in passing, "The body without the spirit is dead" (James 2:26). Despite our best efforts to maintain our health and protect ourselves and our loved ones, the body simply will not cooperate. It dies, and not always at the end of a long and happy life. It dies when three-year-olds drown in bathtubs or people get struck by lightning or hit by cars. It's not just that the body *ultimately* weakens and decays but that it is always at every moment fragile and mortal. This bodily vulnerability has always been contrasted with the soul's supposed immortality and its freedom from embodied fragility. "Despise the flesh," said the fourth-century Greek church father Basil of Caesarea, "for it passes away. See to the welfare of your soul, for it never dies."[3]

We are left with two primary problems to puzzle over in a vision of the person as a body-soul dualism. One is that it appears just about impossible to draw the body-soul distinction without denigrating the former in favor of the latter; without saying, along with Cyril of Alexandria, "The soul is more honorable than the substance of the body."[4] This ultimately becomes degrading to embodied human experience. It also fails to fit with the positive value given to bodily existence in the Bible, which depicts God as Creator of all that is physical and describes this physical existence as good. The second problem is the dualism itself. Its juxtaposition of body against soul seems to suggest a division in the house of the self that does not ring true to our human experience. We know that when our bodies feel pain, it is more than a bodily experience. For that matter, when our soul hurts, we feel it in our body. When we desire sex, we feel it in our soul, not just our body; and when that need is unmet, the same is true. There must be more of an interconnection between body and soul than this dualistic tradition has commonly suggested.

BODY, SOUL, AND SPIRIT

Let's add another layer of complexity by considering a theory that grants the existence of body and soul but adds another entity called "spirit." In this view, human beings have a body, but we also have a nonphysical aspect of the self that is divided up into soul and spirit. The soul is defined as "the experienced self, namely, personality, reason, emotions, and will." The spirit, by contrast, goes deeper. It is "the center of our being, the seat of the self that determines whether we are fundamentally open or closed to God."[5]

At first glance, this may not seem to make as much intuitive sense as the body-soul view. We can observe the body, and most of us sense that there is a spirit in us that is other than the body—we usually call it the soul, though we could label it the spirit without much difficulty. But this new view is asking us to subdivide the "soulish," or nonphysical, dimension of the person into two separate parts, soul and spirit. Why?

One fun way to answer this question is to compare a human being with a cat. Both David Gushee and Fluffy the cat have a body, and the essential features and functions of those bodies are in many ways similar: eating, excreting, copulating, bleeding, breathing, birthing, dying, and so on. (This physical commonality between human and beast is yet another reason, by the way, that the soul has so often been elevated over the body in historic Western thought. Anything that reminds us of our connection as creatures with other creatures has tended to be denigrated.)

Does Fluffy have a soul? Well, if we speak of the soul as the personality, reason, and emotions of a creature, it is hard to deny that to some extent Fluffy has a soul. Anyone who owns more than one cat can tell you that each has its own personality and temperament. This is all the more true of dogs, which differ by breed and also by individual in terms of temperament and personality. It is also hard to deny that animals have and display emotions and that these emotions certainly go beyond raw instinct. The temperament of an animal develops over time, it seems, yet shows some consistency, just as with human beings.

But yet there remains a difference between cats and people. There is a *spiritual* dimension of human beings that goes beyond what we can see in Fluffy or any animal. The spirit is, in contrast to the soul, *the dimension of the self that responds to the transcendent Being who created us.* This spirit is part of what makes us human and is at least part of what it means to have been made in the image of God. Animals do not have a spirit in this sense; we assume that they are unable to pray, worship, reflect, or respond to a transcendent God. On the other hand, if we believe in the angels that are discussed in the Bible, they do have a spirit; indeed, they may be pure spirit, inhabiting bodies only when they need to. So having a spirit is what makes us like the angels, while having a body (and a soul, as defined here) is what makes us like other earthly creatures. We are creatures of heaven *and* creatures of earth, a strange and amazing mix!

If the spirit is the seat of the self, it helps explain some of our internal dynamics. We are certainly all aware of the emotions, thoughts, and desires that flow in and out of our souls—and settle there as the underpinnings of our personality or character. But we also have a deeper spiritual dimension (or, simply, spirit) that has the capacity to examine, comprehend, assess, and transform these dimensions of the self. At the very core of our being is a spirit that wants to shape a self whose experience of thinking, feeling, desiring, reacting, and so on, takes on a particular pattern. We are angry and greedy and we want to be peaceful and giving. We are lustful and lazy and we want to be self-disciplined and hard-working.

The Christian tradition would say that if we are becoming who we should become at the spiritual level, we will want to remove all that is not quite right in us and instead want our soul and its aspects to become more and more like Jesus Christ. The Christian faith also promises that God's Spirit works in our spirit to reshape the patterns of our soul—and our bodily existence, for that matter.

The distinction between spirit and soul is supported in a number of biblical passages. In 1 Thessalonians 5:23, the Apostle Paul closes his letter to the residents of the Christian community of Thessalonica by praying that their "spirit (*pneuma*) and soul (*psyche*) and body (*soma*)" be kept above reproach until Christ returns. In 1 Corinthians 15:45, Paul contrasts Adam and Jesus. Quoting Genesis 2:7, Adam is described as having become "a living being" (*psyche* = soul), whereas "the last Adam," Christ, is a "life-giving spirit" (*pneuma*). And Hebrews 4:12 speaks of the way the Word of God pierces until it divides "soul" (*psyche*) from "spirit" (*pneuma*), penetrating the deepest thoughts and intentions of the heart (*kardia*—which may be understood as another biblical word for the person's spiritual center; it is very often used in this way in the Bible).

One can also go the other direction to make the same point. If a devilish or hateful spirit comes to be our spirit, then it will flow upward, we might say, to permeate thinking, feeling, desiring, and reacting and also therefore the things we do with our bodies. In fact, it is hard to make sense of human evil at its worst without supposing the existence of an infinitely corruptible spiritual center to the human being. For humans like Adolf Hitler and Jeffrey Dahmer, their bodily actions reflected the state of their souls; their souls reflected the deeply corrupted state of their spirits.

It's useful to analyze the aspects of the human self, to gain some sense of the working parts, but does this analysis lose or misplace the essential unity of the human person? Other thinkers, whom we will hear from next, have tackled this question.

ONE IS ALL YOU NEED

The simplest and most radical way to restore an emphasis on a single, unified human being is to deny the existence of any spiritual dimension at all. Steven Pinker, whom we met in

Chapter One, derides the notion of a soul as a premodern "ghost in the machine" concept that cannot survive the findings of modern science. He is convinced that cognitive science has solved the riddle of the mind by reducing mental activity to computational processes occurring in the brain, in tandem with experience and nurture. There is no longer any need to invoke a self or soul that functions as the user of mental processes or even a mind that can be directed by a self to think about one thing or another. Says Pinker, "One can say that the information-processing activity of the brain *causes* the mind, or one can say that it *is* the mind. Every aspect of our mental lives depends entirely on physiological events in the tissues of the brain."[6] Any other belief is an illusion, albeit an illusion fostered by the brain itself, which functions as a "spin doctor" to produce the impression of a "single 'I' in control," an illusion now proven false by studies of the brain itself, according to Pinker.

Likewise, Pinker is impressed by the findings of behavioral genetics. Though he avoids a pure genetic determinism in which we are our DNA and nothing more, Pinker and many like him attribute large proportions of human traits and behavior to genetic causes. Considering personality differences, for example, Pinker argues that "all five of the major personality dimensions are heritable, with perhaps 40 to 50 percent of the variation in a typical population tied to differences in their genes."[7] The same is true of actual behavior, not just temperament. Psychopathic behaviors ranging from "bilking elderly people out of their life savings" to "shooting convenience store clerks lying on the floor during a robbery" are best explained by "genetic predisposition." The choices that we think we are making—the ones we attribute to our self or soul or spirit, may be largely predetermined and could be predicted, as Pinker says, "based on events that took place in your mother's Fallopian tubes decades ago."[8]

Evolutionary psychology, according to Pinker, offers the final blow to the belief in a soul. Using a Darwinian theory of natural selection, Pinker attributes basic human traits and behaviors often credited to the soul or self—such as violence and love, will and conscience—to adaptation in the context of evolution. He concludes, "Love, will, and conscience are in the traditional job description for the soul and have always been placed in opposition to mere 'biological' functions. If those faculties are 'biological' too—that is, evolutionary adaptations implemented in the circuitry of the brain—then the ghost is left with even less to do and might as well be pensioned off for good."[9]

As I said in Chapter One when reflecting on Pinker's approach, there is very little in his view that can be integrated into a Christian perspective. But it is possible to perceive the human being in a way that is informed by contemporary science and yet does not abandon Christian theological convictions or reduce humans to bodies alone.

> *It is possible to perceive the human being in a way that is informed by contemporary science and yet does not abandon Christian theological convictions or reduce humans to bodies alone.*

This alternative view begins at the level of experience. As I think about my wife, Jeanie, for example, the person with whom I have shared life for more than twenty years, it is not my first or

most natural inclination to think of her in two or three parts.
I do not look at her and think, "Here is the body of my wife,
there is the soul of my wife, and just over there is her spirit."
She is one entity, one self, one person with one identity.
When she talks to me, she does so with all aspects of her self:
her hands move, her eyes shine, her head tilts, her mouth
smiles, her mind processes information and communicates it
as she chooses, and her soul or spirit is evident in all of these
actions.

There is no mental act that I have ever watched Jeanie
undertake that does not simultaneously involve her body.
And there is no physical act that does not simultaneously
involve her spirit. Indeed, I would undoubtedly be deeply
unnerved if I ever sensed that Jeanie was "coming apart," that
her body and soul were somehow detaching from each other
rather than remaining inextricably interrelated. That would
be horror movie material. And she would be deeply unnerved if I ever treated her in any way that detached her soul
or spirit from her body. That would be exploitation. What I
do to her body, I do to her soul; what I do to her soul, I do
to her body. Isn't what I've just described a fairly common
experience for most human beings?

The same sort of conclusion is reached when I look
within myself. There is one me, however one may describe
the dimensions of that me. It is not quite accurate just to say
that I have a body. In a very real sense I *am* a body, through
and through. There is no human existence that is not embodied, at least not on this earth.

And however I may describe the different elements or
dimensions of my spiritual side, it is inextricably related to
my body. In fact, honesty compels me to draw a tighter rather
than looser connection between body, soul, and spirit than I
might want to do. For example, it might be nice to blame my

body for overeating or for undisciplined sexual desires. As we saw earlier, this has often been done, much to the disadvantage of the body. But there is no point in any hatred of the body, for it is not the mouth or genitals that are responsible for misconduct; it is the self who chooses to use those organs wrongly. As Jesus put it, "It is from within, from the human heart, that evil intentions come" (Mark 7:21). A monistic understanding of the self refuses to pit body against soul but instead sees that a single *embodied self* is responsible for all actions.

Many elements of the biblical account also seem to point in the direction of a single unified self. In the creation story, for example, we are told that "the Lord God formed man from the dust of the ground, and breathed into his nostrils the breath of life, and the man became a living being" (Genesis 2:7). The man (Hebrew, *adam*) is formed out of the ground (Hebrew, *adamah*), establishing the intimate connection between humanity and the earthly materials from which we come. We are flesh, we emerge from flesh, we live enfleshed, we die as flesh, and we are returned to the ground from which we came. God gives life to us by breathing life into us—the soil-creature, one might say, is animated by the breath of God, and so we live until that animation ceases and we return to the soil. But this does not make us dualistic selves. A living human being is a physical-spiritual creature in a single self—a psychosomatic (soul-body) unity, as it is sometimes put.

But if this is the case, what happens when we die? Unlike the Greek notion that the body decays while the self floats off to heaven, a biblical (especially a Jewish) understanding seems to envision no such separable existence between body and soul or spirit. When we die, all of us dies. If there is to be any continued existence after death, it will have to be in a reanimated or re-created body that God simply chooses to make alive again. This is how Paul put it in 1 Thessalonians 4:14–16: "Since we believe that Jesus died and rose again, even so, through Jesus, God will bring with him those who have died [Greek, *koimethentas,* literally 'fallen asleep']. For this we declare to you by the word of the Lord, that we who are alive, who are left behind until the coming of the Lord, will by no means precede those who have died. For the Lord himself . . . will descend from heaven, and the dead in Christ will rise first."

The nature of this resurrected body is very difficult for us to understand or describe. Paul depicts it as a spiritual body, an imperishable kind of body that will never taste death again (1 Corinthians 15:35–53). And yet it is a body, and it maintains continuity with the earthly body that was either buried in the ground when we died or, if we are alive when Jesus comes, will be transformed in the process of the ultimate transfiguration of all things (15:52–54). The historic Christian creeds all envision the "resurrection of the body, and the life everlasting," but this is a belief that has subtly faded in the past few centuries in the direction of a body-soul dualism in which the immortal soul goes to heaven and the body is left entirely behind.[10]

This leaves a final problem for a unified view of the self, at least from a biblical perspective. What are we to make of the various labels given in the Bible to the spiritual part of the self? As we have seen in the sketch of other views, there certainly are biblical references to the soul or spirit, not to mention the mind, heart, emotions, will, and so on. These references cannot merely be dismissed.

Biblical vocabulary for the spirit or soul denotes *aspects, dimensions,* or *facets* of the one self, rather than fundamental distinctions within a multipart self. The Bible knows and communicates that there is a spiritual dimension to human persons and in various contexts labels these dimensions in various ways. For example, Jesus calls his listeners to love God with all their heart, soul, mind, and strength (Mark 12:30). Just as no one seriously suggests that the self be divided into these four elements, so we should not subdivide the human self using any other scheme (even those devised from various biblical accounts). We are one self, with various facets almost too mysterious to name, and with the whole of this one self we are to worship and serve the one God.

ONE IN THREE, THREE IN ONE

The Christian tradition has at its very heart a model of self-hood that is simultaneously unified and multipart: the Trinity. The historic Nicene Creed, recited to this day in many churches around the world, begins, "We believe in one God." But then it moves on to describe this God as Father Almighty, only begotten Son Jesus Christ, and life-giving Holy Spirit. God is one, as the Scripture declares: "Hear, O Israel, the Lord our God, the Lord is one" (Deuteronomy 6:4, NIV). Affirmation of the profound oneness of God, over against all forms of the world of many gods that dominated the other cultures of ancient Near East, lies at the heart of biblical faith. There is one God alone, and only this God may be worshiped.

And yet Christian faith affirms that this one God is three Persons: Father, Son, and Holy Spirit. Christian tradition has wrestled mightily to make sense of how one God could be three Persons; how three Persons could be one God. Yet the biblical record, especially the New Testament, demanded that the church find a way to describe a God in three Persons, for the person and work of all three could be found delineated in Scripture itself. We will say much more about this issue in Chapter Three. For now, suffice it to say that the end result was a remarkably rich, deeply paradoxical belief in an eternally existing God who brought life into the universe through the mystery and majesty of creation.

Christians have within our faith the resources, then, to believe that a personal entity can be simultaneously one and three, three and one. More precisely, the church has taught that God is simultaneously *one in three* and *three in one*. If this is true about God, could it also be true about human beings? Is it not possible that a triune God would create triune creatures as the pinnacle of his creative efforts?

> *The church has taught that God is simultaneously one in three and three in one. If this is true about God, could it also be true about human beings?*

Following a line of thinking Augustine of Hippo pursued in the fourth century, I propose that we might think of the human person as a three-in-one, one-in-three entity. Whereas Augustine described these three components of the self as *memory, understanding, and will,* I want to claim that the self consists of *body, soul, and spirit.* As God designed us, we are truly one self, one person, one entity. Any sense that we have of a fundamental internal war within us—any to-the-core internal division we sense within ourselves—bears witness to the catastrophic effects of sin on human life and the deep need for repair of the human person. When people sense themselves "coming apart" or "at war with themselves," they are in real trouble. (We will look at this in more depth in a later chapter.) But as designed by

God, we were intended as a single whole, a united person; although we have this wholeness as our heritage, we are constantly journeying toward its full realization. Indeed, it is appropriate to say that the integration of the various aspects of our one self is a key part of what life's journey is all about. So we are one and must be one. Yet we are also three: body, soul, and spirit. How can we unpack this mystery further to understand it better? We can start with the *spirit,* the deepest core and spiritual center of the human being. It is, as noted earlier, the transcendent dimension of the self that responds to the transcendent Being who created us. The soul consists of the rational, emotional, psychological, temperamental, and other distinctive internal features of the human person. And the body can continue to be defined as the physical structure and material substance of the human being.

While these distinctions can legitimately be drawn, this must be done without ever collapsing into three distinct and separate parts. If the person is three in one, then body, soul, and spirit constantly intertwine. We are embodied souls and ensouled bodies; we are embodied spirits and inspirited bodies; likewise, we are ensouled spirits and inspirited souls. We must emphasize our oneness at least as much as we emphasize our threeness—probably more.

Here we enter the realm of mystery. Christians have always affirmed that the personal identity of God is a deep mystery; here we see (and should we be surprised?) that the personal identity of the human beings he has made is also deeply mysterious. We are, after all, made in the image of God. Our minds bump up against their limits, and our words fail us. It begins to be much easier to say it wrong than to say it right, to know what we must *not* affirm rather than what we must affirm.

The mystery is only deepened when we realize that each of the three dimensions of the one self I am proposing here can also be subdivided further. It is easy to see this when we think about our bodies, which consist of at least six different systems (circulatory, respiratory, genitourinary, musculoskeletal, digestive, and nervous) and can be analyzed at ever more minute levels of examination, down to our genetic materials and their constituent elements.

A careful examination of the elements of what I am calling the soul yields the same result. We can speak of an individual's mind or intellect, emotions, personality, temperament, imagination, interests, skills, gifts, and vitality or strength. These aspects interrelate intimately. And each of these elements can be broken down into constituent parts. For example, it is possible to identify a wide range of particular intellectual abilities and processes (empirical observation and description, rational deduction and induction, logic, imagination, problem solving, computation, and so on), with individuals varying considerably in their gifts, training, and skills.

If we draw a tentative boundary line between soul and spirit, as I am suggesting, this leaves the spirit as the seat of the self's fundamental orientation to God, to neighbor, and to self. I draw these categories from Jesus' answer when asked to name the greatest commandment of the Jewish Law. He said, "You shall love the Lord your God with all your heart, and with all your soul, and with all your mind. . . . And you shall love your neighbor as yourself" (Matthew 22:37, 39). The core questions for each human being are all embedded here. What is my stance toward the God who made me and sustains me and to whom I shall return? What is my stance toward the neighbors around me? What is my stance toward myself? The answers to these questions about God, neighbor, and self will determine the shape of my *will* (what I choose, what I strive for, what I am inclined to do, the way I exercise internal control over my soul and my body), my *character* (the aggregate of "soulish" features and traits that characterize my thinking, feeling, willing, and acting), and my *heart* (the center of my total personality and selfhood, "where the person decides for or against God").[11] Jesus calls his listeners to love God, neighbor, and self and to establish love as the direction of the will, the shape of the character, and the inclination of the heart. Whether it is love, hate, or indifference, some fundamental orientation will characterize the human spirit, the seat of the trinitarian self. We had better choose it wisely.

Thus my conception of human identity consists of three concentric realms—of the body, soul, and spirit—united as one, as depicted in Figure 2.2.

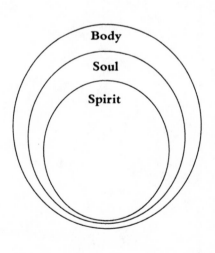

BODY
Circulatory
Respiratory
Musculoskeletal
Nervous, Genitourinary
Digestive

SOUL
Mind/Intellect
Emotions
Personality
Temperament
Imagination, Vitality

SPIRIT
Orientation to: God,
Neighbor, Self
Will
Heart
Character

Figure 2.2

There is yet one more way in which the human self is simultaneously one thing and more than one. When I fall in love, I am me and she is she but together we are something new. We are simultaneously two and yet one. When we marry and have a child, I am me and she is she and baby makes three—and yet all are one, a family. The trinitarian mystery of human identity deepens all the more when we consider the relationships we are embedded in and the loves with which we are blessed. This subject—the social character of the self—will be the subject of Chapter Three. It is a fundamental aspect of the human nature we carry with us on our journey toward wholeness.

3

Why Do Relationships Matter So Much to Me?

Do not live entirely isolated, having retreated
into yourselves . . . but gather instead to seek
the common good together.
— EPISTLE OF BARNABAS, SECOND-CENTURY
TEACHER AND WRITER

Just before beginning this chapter, I had a two-day argument with my wife, Jeanie, over a thorny issue that had troubled us for some time. In the midst of this argument, I noticed how it was affecting me: I couldn't sleep well, I had headaches, I was distracted, and my stomach hurt.

I also noticed how the argument was affecting my relationships with my children. I had a hard time finding the energy to relate to them. I couldn't focus on what they were saying to me. Our time together as a family felt unappealing and unpleasant, which is far from the joy I usually feel when I'm with them. I could also hardly muster the energy to get any work done.

There was nowhere I could go and nothing I could do to make the misery of this unresolved argument go away— other than finally tackling the problem head on. The only way to feel better was finally to apologize and begin the process of reconciliation. When Jeanie and I hugged for the first time in two days, I breathed a deep sigh of relief as much of the built up tension melted away. My whole body relaxed. My headache soon went away. My stomach stopped hurting. And I felt immediately much more prepared to care for my children and to return to my work.

Perhaps I am a wimp when it comes to marital conflict. Blessedly, our marriage is very peaceful most of the time, and so I have not, like others I know, had to become accustomed to living in a state of alienation from my wife. Maybe that's why I'm even more vulnerable to all kinds of maladies when things do go wrong.

Yet I think there is much more to it than that. Just as there is a link between body and soul in this story—when my soul hurt, my body did as well—there is also a link between an important relationship that is hurting the rest of me, body and soul. In fact, the relationship pain, as it might be called, temporarily weakened my ability to relate to other loved ones in my own family.

Could it be that just as the human being is made up of interwoven yet invisible strands of body, soul, and spirit coalescing to make one self, the human being is also invisibly interconnected to other people just as profoundly? We cannot "see" the human soul or spirit, but we know they are there. Similarly, we cannot see the ties that bind one human being to another as we progress, alone and together, on life's journey. Just as we are more than the bodies we can see,

> *Just as we are more than the bodies we can see, we are more than our individual, separate selves.*

we are more than our individual, separate selves. The cords of connection that bind us one to another are part of that "something more."

This chapter explores the idea that we as humans are intrinsically social and that our journeys are undertaken in community. We exist in relationships from the very beginning of our lives, and human life apart from such relationships would cease to be recognizably human. The question of why relationships matter so much is best answered by looking at the way that our social ties with other people—and with God—help define what it means to be human. Just as we cannot survive without oxygen, we cannot survive without relationships. Just as we cannot picture a human being who is all body and no soul, so we cannot picture a human being who is a solitary self without relationships. We will see that this is not just intuitively true but an important part of the Christian tradition.

WE ARE OUR RELATIONSHIPS

We live in a culture that celebrates individualism. From our very beginnings as a nation, we have emphasized personal privacy, individual liberty, freedom of conscience, and the "pursuit of happiness" as each person defines that elusive goal. The hero who goes it alone, who stands against the crowd, who picks up stakes and moves on to greener pastures or new frontiers is part of our national mythology. Readers of a certain generation will think of square-jawed Gary Cooper as Sheriff Kane in *High Noon* or perhaps James Bond, Rambo, or some role played by Bruce Willis.

There is much to be said for this grand old American tradition, a tradition rooted in much broader intellectual

currents in the Western world. In its own way, it was a re-
action to the excesses of an Old World vision of community,
in which there was little personal privacy, liberty, mobility, or
freedom of conscience. Few of us today would willingly
choose to live in the societies from which America's early set-
tlers emerged.

However, this individualism, now so deeply engrained
in the American soul and culture, obscures our intrinsic need
for relationships with each other. Regardless of the assump-
tions of individualism, most of us recognize that we are social
creatures, bound to one another through various relationships
in various kinds of communities. Perhaps the many great evils
that human beings have done to each other in recent decades,
like the Holocaust and Stalin's prison camps, have caused our
most sensitive thinkers to notice once again how bound we
are to each other, how much we need each other, how vulnerable we are to each other, and how disastrous it is when
we forget these connections, needs, and vulnerabilities.

Even some Christian conceptions of the nature of God
and his relationship with human beings has been colored by
this persistent cultural emphasis on individualism. For many
Christians, God is a deity who is all alone, by himself, presid-
ing over the universe. This God is often pictured as a rather
remote and stern judge or ruler who alone knows, decides,
judges, and directs all things. This is God the self-sufficient,
omniscient, all-powerful, solitary king. It is a powerfully important image for God that is embedded in our cultural
imagination.

Subtly related to this image of the solitary God is an
image of the solitary human being to whom this God relates.
A God who is alone looks down upon the earth and sees *me*
and six billion other *me*'s, all of whom he relates to in soli-
tude. This is a God who has six billion individual relation-

ships, whether as fearsome and angry Judge or as loving Father or as kindly Grandfather—but in any case, this is a God whom we think of as relating not to communities but only to solitary selves.

This vision of a solitary deity seems to be a particularly Protestant rendering of God, deeply influenced by a certain tradition of interpreting the Old Testament as well as a certain kind of Western individualism. As a Protestant for the last twenty-five years, this depiction of God is easy for me to describe because I have heard countless sermons, prayers, and conversations based on it. As I look back further, however, to my Catholic childhood, I recall a very different vision of the divine realm. In the Catholic imagination, God has much company in heaven, with Jesus at his right hand; Mary, the "Mother of God," looking on maternally; thousands of saints among the throng around the throne; and hosts of glorious angels. This Catholic vision of God is, to put it mildly, much more social than the working Protestant version. It offers a veritable riot of relationships in the heavenly throne room. We are not here trying to decide which of these visions of God and his relationship to the world and human beings is accurate, only to point out the centrality of relationship, even in an individualistic culture.

In fact, our need for others begins even before we are born. No human being begins life through any choice of his or her own. Human beings are conceived through the most intimate form of community that exists on the planet—sexual intercourse between a man and a woman. At its best, the conception of a child is an outcome of the love that exists between two people, a love that has drawn them out of isolation into the closest of unions. When a couple "make love" and do so with openness to conceiving a child, they are simultaneously expressing the love that they share, deepening that love through the intimacy of sexual intercourse, and making themselves available for the creation of new life. *Making love makes life,* and (until the test-tube baby boom) no human being has come into this world apart from this act of interpersonal communion. So much is really going on in the very earthy act of sexual intercourse that we can see why the world's moral traditions have always tried to guard its boundaries with such care.

Newborn children remain radically dependent on the men and women whose lovemaking brought them into this world, even if those who conceived the child abdicate their responsibility. Someone must care for each helpless baby, and that care sets the stage for all the relationships that follow, for good or for ill. No child survives to adulthood apart from community of some sort, whether the community of biological mother or father or some other community as a substitute or supplement. The complete helplessness of the infant, the relative helplessness of the child, and even the complex dependence of the adolescent require a long-term investment on the part of some kind of caregiving community.

Even when adolescents begin that awkward transition in orientation away from their families to their peers, they are actually shifting from one kind of social allegiance to another rather than abandoning community per se. It is a perilous transition, and it can become disastrous for adolescents who do not connect to a meaningful and constructive peer group community. They can sink into the despair that comes from social isolation, or even worse, they can associate with a whole range of destructive peer groups. This was the terrible path taken by Columbine High School killers Dylan Klebold and Eric Harris. They went from a sense of social rejection by the main group of their peers at school into a newfound sense of being a community of two—two vengeful killers, that is.

Beginning in adolescence and extending into young adulthood (and often far beyond), most human beings search for a romantic life partner. This is another (enjoyable yet challenging) quest for community, in this case the community that marks the transition from one generation to the next and prepares the way for new life yet again. When successful, the mating process leads to new kinds of community, as families form, children are born, and new extended family relationships develop.

Adults of course create other kinds of communities and relationships beyond their families. We create, dissolve, and re-create an amazing variety of communities, from the most intimate friendships to shared-interest associations like book clubs and bridge clubs and motorcycle clubs, social service and volunteer networks, sports teams, business enterprises, restaurants and bars, schools of every type, military units, religious bodies, ethnic groups, nations, and societies, and governments at many levels. When we think about all of these kinds of communities, it is hard to imagine that there are human beings who are *not* involved in multiple relationship networks every day of their lives, even in the remotest areas of the world. Intimacy and proximity vary across these communities and relationships, but they all involve us in a network of association with one another.

Many streams of contemporary thought have concluded that human beings are "radically social and interdependent" and that there is no "individuality" that is not socially constructed.[1] It's not just that individuals choose to associate in communities but that there really is no such thing as an individual who is not embedded in such communities. We literally *do not know who we are* apart from our relationships with others. And throughout life, the self is arduously formed (and to some extent always being formed), gaining coherence, stability, and permanence of identity through its engagements with other people.

The different community contexts that have shaped us provide a map by which we can locate ourselves coherently and cohesively. I am the only son of David E. Gushee and Jay Gushee, who come from Boston and Altoona and whose lineage stretches back in a particular direction across the Atlantic. I am the older brother of three younger sisters, Alice, Janette, and Katey. I grew up in Vienna, Virginia, during the 1960s and 1970s. I became a committed Christian at the age of sixteen and joined Providence Baptist Church. I attended the Fairfax County Public Schools and then the College of William and Mary before graduate school in Kentucky and New York. I met and married the adorable Jeanie Grant from Falls Church, Virginia, whose parents hail from Georgia and Florida and whose lineage also stretches back in a particular direction. I am the natural father of three children and adoptive father of one grown child. I am a member of a Southern Baptist church and serve as a professor at a Tennessee Baptist university. I belong to half a dozen professional organizations to which I feel various degrees of loyalty. I read certain magazines and listen to certain kinds of radio stations. I know who I am because I can map my identity on this multi-dimensional grid whose axes are formed by these various markers of identity in community. All of us could offer a comparable personal map that reveals how profoundly community shapes the identities we carry with us on our journey through life.

The extraordinary importance of our relationships is never more obvious than when they are disrupted. We go to great lengths to prevent such disruptions or to ease their effects, and we suffer when we are separated—voluntarily or involuntarily—from those to whom we are closest.

When we are geographi-
cally separated from those we
love, we often feel the pain of that
separation as if it were a physical
pain. As I wrote the first draft of
this chapter, my baby girl, my
eleven-year-old daughter Marie,
was away at a weeklong sports
camp, about six hours distant.
This was her first time away at
camp—and our first time away
from her. There was no way to

> *The extraordinary
> importance of
> our relationships
> is never more
> obvious than
> when they are
> disrupted.*

keep in touch with her; the best we could do to stay connected was to write two notes in advance for her to read at
intervals during her week away. I felt her absence in my bones,
and so did her mother. I did not feel quite whole again until
I saw her.

We also feel great pain at transitions in our lives, when
people we have loved are moving away. I am often surprised
to see just how painful it is for many parents when their children go off to college. I am not quite to that stage in life yet,
but it is coming very quickly. I can imagine that the excited
eighteen-year-old is pretty clueless, as she drives off to her
next great adventure, that this is one of her parents' saddest
days. All three are experiencing a transition in their relationship, and it will never again be quite the same. One of the
costs of our highly mobile culture is the toll it takes on us as
we end relationships and are forced to reconstitute new ones,
over and over again. Something like 15 or 20 percent of the
American population moves every year.

If temporary physical separation is difficult, the loss of
relationship when someone dies is the ultimate sorrow.
Mourning over another's death is one of the universal human

practices, regardless of the form grief takes across cultures. And there is a special kind of unspeakable grief reserved for those who are denied the opportunity to properly mourn their own dead, as with those who lost family during the Holocaust or the 2004 Indian Ocean tsunami disaster. When mourning is allowed to proceed properly, we notice the great care that is taken with the body of the dead, the elaborate rituals of remembrance and sorrow, the hope articulated in so many faiths of reuniting some day in an afterlife. All point to our dependence on relationships and to the *particularity* of this dependence. We don't just need relationships in general; we cherish particular relationships that develop with particular and ultimately irreplaceable human beings. And when we bury certain key people in our lives, we struggle to figure out who we are now that this person is no longer around. One thinks of the many widows who lose spouses after fifty or more years of marriage and seem entirely disoriented for a long time, perhaps for the rest of their lives. Some simply lose the will to live and die of a broken heart.

Such profound grief only reinforces the claim that we are persons in community and that, as the philosopher John Macmurray writes (paraphrasing Acts 17:28), "We live and move and have our being not in ourselves but in one another."[2] Even our language points to this intertwining of selves when people say of exceptionally close friends, "It was hard to tell where one left off and the other began."

The German pastor and theologian Dietrich Bonhoeffer sensed the same thing when imprisoned in Nazi Germany. He worried about the fate of his family and friends daily. In a September 1943 letter to his parents just after fierce Allied bombing hit Berlin, he wrote:

It's remarkable how we think at such times about the people that we should not like to live without, and almost or entirely forget about ourselves. It is only then that we feel how closely our own lives are bound up with other people's, and in fact how the center of our own lives is outside ourselves, and how little we are separate entities. The "as though it were a part of me" is perfectly true, as I have often felt after hearing that one of my colleagues or pupils had been killed. I think it is a literal fact of nature that human life extends far beyond our physical existence.[3]

The same point is made quite beautifully in the Bible when marriage is described as a "one-flesh relationship" (Genesis 2:18–25; Matthew 19:1–12). Jesus says of the married couple, "They are no longer two, but one flesh" (Matthew 19:6). You cannot physically look at two exceptionally close people and see the extent to which their two bodies and selves have become one, but in another sense you can see it nonetheless, provoking either admiration or envy, depending on how your own relationships are doing.

Of course, any mention of the "one flesh" marriage relationship, especially in our day, reminds us of the intense pain of broken relationships. Relationships are fragile, and yet we often seem perversely determined to mess them up. Woven as tightly as they are into our lives, any stress on these relationships becomes a stress on the self at its very core. And any collapse of a key relationship becomes a crisis for the self. In fact, it can and often does become (as with divorce) the occasion when we feel that our very self has died and needs to be reconstructed.

For divorcing adults, especially those whose "one-fleshness" is pretty far along, despite their problems, because they have been together for a while, divorce is as physically painful as if someone had taken a hacksaw and forcibly cut the two intertwined selves apart. Children caught in divorce are especially vulnerable: because a child generally identifies as the child of Mom and Dad, who love each other and are married to each other and live with the child at a particular address, divorce often causes a shattering of identity. After divorce, the child is still the product of Mom and Dad, but they now no longer love each other, are no longer married, no longer live with each other and together with the child, no longer are "one flesh." As the enfleshed embodiment of their parents' love, children of divorce may experience it as a split in their very selves.[4] No wonder both adults and children respond to divorce with such visceral and profound emotions as rage, hatred, and despair.

Despite our yearning for relationships, not all of us have them, for any number of reasons. Some of us are isolated; others are not alone but are still lonely, even in a crowd. The physical presence of other human beings in our space does not mean that we are emotionally connected to any of them. It is even possible to be lonely or to feel isolated within intimate relationships that are temporarily or chronically estranged. The only thing worse than being lonely and alone is being lonely and not alone.

> *The only thing worse than being lonely and alone is being lonely and not alone.*

But think especially for a moment about the person who is genuinely all alone in the world. I think of the middle-aged woman I knew whose parents were dead, whose brothers lived far away and had rejected her, and who was in and out of jobs due to a variety of factors. Until she made the effort to find Christian community in our local church, she lived her life in near-total isolation. She sometimes spent her holidays alone. She "celebrated" her birthday alone. How many millions of people live miserable lives of loneliness and isolation? Life lived in such a way is the exact opposite of our intrinsic human need for relationship. It is not surprising that the lonely person, sitting in the deserted diner on Christmas morning eating by herself, is one of the ultimate symbols of human misery.

That kind of social isolation is a dead end, and yet it is the logical end result of many trends in our culture, including our misguided celebration of the rugged individual who goes it alone. But this vision of life simply does not fit with what we can observe, nor does it fit with human nature. We are social creatures, as we can see when our relationships flourish and when they fail. The resources of the Christian tradition are designed to deepen and reinforce this conviction.

CREATION, COVENANT, AND LOVE

From its very beginning, the Bible depicts human beings as social creatures who need various forms of community throughout their life journeys in order to fulfill God's plan for their lives. Indeed, even once the human relationship with God goes badly astray, God uses community to repair it.

In the biblical account, the initial relationship that exists on the planet is between God and the first man, Adam. It is striking to note this line from Genesis 2: "It is not good that the man should be alone; I will make him a helper as his partner" (2:18). Up to this point in the creation narrative, everything has been described as "good" or "very good," but now here is something that is not good—a human being in isolation. Even though this human being has unhindered access to God, he remains "alone"—*and that is not good*. This is quite an astonishing acknowledgment of the indispensability of human relationships in our lives. Even the divine-human relationship cannot take its place. It would be good to remember this whenever we are tempted to tell lonely people that all they need, or should need, is God. God himself recognized that this wasn't true! And look at how God, the ultimate in self-sufficiency (as we tend to think), created people and wanted a relationship with each one, from the very beginning.

So God creates Eve, who becomes the first wife, before the second chapter of Genesis even reaches its conclusion. The community that exists between man and woman, as husband and wife, is thus depicted in the Bible as the basic form of human community. From this divinely ordained union, consummated in sexual intercourse, come Cain and Abel, the children who then turn the first couple into the first family (Genesis 4:1–2), though it doesn't take long before one of them (Cain) kills the other (Abel). Generations ensue and human beings slowly spread across the earth. Eventually, God is angered by human sin and sends the flood (6–8), sparing only Noah and his family. But once again from this new first family come descendants who spread out across the earth. Genesis 10 offers a kind of primeval geography lesson in which the various descendants of Noah are placed in their particular regions across the known world. Even as it becomes ever more diverse in geographical location, culture, and eventually language, the human family springs from a pair of common ancestors. And the God who created the first humans and placed them in the first marriage remains committed to relating to the entire human family and to being acknowledged by all as the sovereign Creator God.

By Genesis 12, the human family exists as a geographically dispersed array of tribes and nations, worshiping different gods whom they understand and misunderstand in various ways even as they eke out an existence on the earth. Even that early on, many of the forms of human community that remain with us to this day are in place: couples, families, tribes or peoples, communities, and societies, sometimes organized as primitive states.

We also see plenty of evidence both that God seeks to relate to the entire human family and that human beings have difficulty properly understanding God or God's will or intentions for them. Thus Genesis 12 introduces the figure of Abram (later called Abraham) the Mesopotamian and records the call from God for this man and his family to leave their homeland and found a new nation.

At this pivotal fork in the road of divine-human history, God promises to make a covenant (essentially an exchange of sacred and binding promises and obligations) with Abraham. God promises a number of things to Abram and his line: to show him and then give him a particular land (Genesis 12:1), to give him many descendants who will become a great nation, to make his (family) name great, to bless those who bless him and curse those who curse him (12:2–3), and to make him a blessing to others (12:2). In fact, in a critically important promise, God says, "In you all the families of the earth shall be blessed" (12:3). Abram's binding obligation in return is to believe God's promises and follow his direction.

In this story are the beginnings of the journey of human salvation. God chooses a man and his family as the starting point for a special relationship with a chosen people, later to be called Israel. This relationship will be structured as a covenant, in which God promises special provision and direction for his covenanted people in return for their exclusive loyalty and obedience both to God and to the specific provisions of his will.

From nearly the beginning, then, in Scripture two central concepts—creation and covenant—are emphasized. God creates human beings and makes covenants with them in order to bring them (back) into a relationship with him and into conformity with his will. God's goal in creation is to make creatures who will freely worship him, serve him, obey him, and do his will in relation to one another and the rest of the created order. After sin corrupts the human experience and disrupts human relationships at every level, God does not give up but instead acts to reclaim his world.

But the way God does this is through the formation of covenant community. God does not call Abraham alone but instead his family and eventually the entire Israelite people. Thus God reclaims the world through community, by selecting one people to whom he will relate most intensively and whom he will direct. They will then serve as a witness to others.

In God's relationship with the Hebrew people, he pays detailed attention to all aspects of community experience. The summary declaration of all spiritual and moral obligations, the Ten Commandments, offers four fundamental obligations in relation to God and six in relation to neighbors. The Torah, or Mosaic Law, contains detailed prescriptions for family life, business affairs, political organization, conflict resolution, and criminal law, in addition to regulations related to worship and religious festivities. The Torah envisions Israel as a community characterized by social justice as a reflection of their commitment to a just God who redeemed them from the injustice of slavery in Egypt.

It is easy to get lost in the details of the hundreds of laws one finds in the Torah or Pentateuch (the first five books of the Hebrew Bible or, as Christians call it, the Old Testament).

But it helps to remember that all the laws are about how a people chosen by God can live in a way pleasing to him, which includes community life. And the big picture is that God prescribes this way of life for Israel ultimately as a way of reaching the rest of the world and restoring the nations to "right relationship" with their Creator.

The New Testament declares that Jesus Christ is the culmination of God's plan to redeem the world. Not only does Jesus offer a riveting and authoritative interpretation of the Jewish moral tradition that invites all his listeners to live out God's revealed will, but his brutal death also serves as an atoning sacrifice for human sins that opens Israel's covenant with God to the people of all the world. Henceforth the community of those who are committed to serving God (to being in right relationship with him) is extended to people from every tribe, race, language, and nation (Acts 1:8). The Christian church becomes a new global community of those who seek to live in obedience to the God of Abraham, Isaac, and Jacob. God's promise to Abraham ("In you all the families of the earth will be blessed") is thus fulfilled in a new way.

Jesus taught his followers that *love of God* and *love of neighbor* are the greatest of the commandments. He told his most intimate disciples that they must love each other, that this is the "new commandment" (John 13:34). As the Roman Catholic Catechism has put it, "Charity [love] is the greatest social commandment."[5] God creates human beings as an expression of divine love, with the intention that we will both love our Creator and love our fellow creatures. What is this love? Love is best understood as a decision to bind oneself to and seek the flourishing of another person or object. When we love God, we bind ourselves to him in every way we can and seek to bring him pleasure with our lives. When we love others, we also bind ourselves to them, and we seek in every way we can to help them flourish. Such love is the most precious commodity to be found on this planet. It is social glue; it binds creatures to each other and inclines them to honor and value one another against the pressures of all forces that would cause us to reject and harm each other.

God's way of teaching human beings what he designed us to be and shepherding us into a way of life that more closely reflects that design is through the making of covenants that structure relationships so that love will be advanced through the discipline of obedience to rules and fidelity to promises. The Bible is realistic about the way sin has disrupted human nature and broken relationships at every level that were supposed to be loving and harmonious.

Covenant thus becomes a scaffolding for the building and rebuilding of love in any kind of community. In making covenants, God is implicitly and sometimes explicitly acknowledging how difficult it is for us to get it right. In such covenants, we learn over and over how to obey God's deepest intentions for humanity—to love him and to love our neighbors.

In the Christian view, when Jesus returns and history comes to an end, those who have lived in covenant with him will finally be able to love without hindrance—as God designed in creation and as God has demanded in every covenant he has ever made with human beings. At that time, love will be complete and the universe will no longer be marred by broken relationships of any kind. The Bible here offers a profound depiction of what many people long for without even knowing it—an end to the alienation and brokenness that so pervades human life. No wonder that "Come, Lord Jesus," was one of the most popular prayers in the early church. Come, Lord Jesus, and bring healing to our broken relationships, and our broken hearts. . . .

IN THE IMAGE OF
GOD'S RELATIONSHIPS

One of the most interesting and fruitful ways of understanding the centrality of relationships as part of God's essential and eternal nature is through an exploration of the Trinity and the relationships among God the Father, God the Son Jesus Christ, and God the Holy Spirit. If we can come to a better understanding of the relationships among the Trinity, we might just gain some extraordinary insights into our own nature as well; because, after all, the Bible says we are made in the image of God (Genesis 1:27).

The Trinity has always been one of the greatest and holiest mysteries in Christian thought. In fact, it is far easier to get it wrong than it is to get it right. Though it is clear that God is depicted as Father, Son, and Holy Spirit in Scripture, it took centuries of reflection for the Christian church to arrive at anything approaching consensus on how to articulate the concept of the Trinity. And that reflection is still going on. When theologians say that God is Triune (literally, three-one), they mean that God is social in his very nature. There is one God, the Christian creeds affirm, and the unity of this one God is absolute.

> *Scripture speaks primarily of the roles that each person of God plays* in relation to human salvation—*the Father sends the Son to redeem the world he has created, the Son lives and dies for the world, and the Spirit draws people to salvation.*

And yet this God is described in Scripture as three persons, Father, Son, and Holy Spirit. Scripture speaks primarily of the roles that each person of God plays *in relation to human salvation*—the Father sends the Son to redeem the world he has created, the Son lives and dies for the world, and the Spirit draws people to salvation. But the Bible also points to the holy internal life of God, of the Trinity. This is extraordinarily mysterious. We are only given glimpses.

The creeds affirm that the one and only Son is "eternally begotten of the Father," of one being and one substance with the Father. The fully divine Son also became human through his incarnation, suffered, died, and was raised on our behalf, to win us salvation from our sins. The Western church (as opposed to the Eastern Orthodox tradition) affirms that the Holy Spirit eternally proceeds from the Father and the Son, meaning that the Spirit always has been, is, and always will be flowing out of the very existence of the Father and the Son— kind of like the good and vital "spirit" that flows out of a joyful relationship between a husband and wife over many years. The whole church affirms that the Spirit plays a leading role in teaching, inspiring, and sustaining God's people today, ever since Christ's resurrection and ascension into heaven.

There have been all kinds of debates about whether the three persons of the Trinity emerged in any kind of succession or chronological order. It is easy to think of the solitary Father being first, choosing then to beget the Son, and then the Spirit proceeding from Father and Son together. But Scripture describes an *eternal* relationship among Father, Son, and Spirit. From before Creation, the church affirms, God existed in three persons. There never was a time when he was not three persons. Father, Son, and Spirit were present at Creation (Genesis 1:26–28; Proverbs 8; Colossians 1:15); they have been in relationship since "before the foundation of the world" (John 17:24). Yet there have been historical stages in God's relationship with humanity, including the decisive stage in which God as the Son took on human nature in Jesus of Nazareth, and the succeeding (and still current) stage in which the Spirit has been poured out upon the church. In my view, it is correct to say that his interaction with humanity has affected God—for example, in the Incarnation, God for the first time takes human nature into his divine nature through the experience of Jesus the Son. It is even proper to acknowledge that the three persons of the one God have related in dynamic and varying ways to the world at different stages, even while eternally coexisting as Father, Son, and Spirit.

At times in Scripture we are given glimpses into the quality of the relationship of Father, Son, and Spirit. At least in terms of the Father-Son connection, this is perhaps nowhere depicted more sublimely than in Jesus' prayer in John 17, one of the most exalted and, yes, dazzling sections of the Bible. You almost have to cover your eyes to read this chapter, it's so bright with the presence of God. In this lengthy prayer, Jesus is depicting the internal relational dynamic within the Trinity as involving endless mutual self-giving, a delighted deflection of attention to one another, and joyful love. The followers of Jesus are described as the blessed recipients of the overflow of this love, who then were and still even now are beginning to participate in this same quality of relationship that exists within the Father-Son bond.

In this complex chapter of John's Gospel, one sees the pattern for the relationships within the Trinity: The Father glorifies the Son and the Son glorifies the Father (John 17: 1, 4–5). The Father gives authority to the Son and the Son uses that authority to do the Father's will (17:2). The Father

gives Jesus authority over human beings, and Jesus uses that
access to people to offer the Father's salvation to them (17:2,
6, 9). The Father sends the Son, and the Son prays that people
will know the Father through him (17:3). The Father gives
the Son the words to speak; the Son gives those words to his
followers, who know that neither the words nor the Son
come from the Son himself but from the Father who sent
him (17:7–8). All of the Son's disciples are the Father's, and
the Father's are the Son's, and the Son has been glorified in
them (17:10). The Father gave the Son his name, which pro-
tected the Son and which he now deploys in order to protect
the disciples (17:11). The Son prays that the disciples may be
one as the Father and the Son are one (17:11, 20, 22, 23). The
Son is in the Father and the Father is in the Son, and Jesus
prays that the disciples may be in them (17:21). The Father
gives the Son glory, and the Son gives the disciples this glory
(17:22). The Father has loved the Son since before Creation
(17:24), and Jesus has passed this love on to the disciples so
that it is now in them (17:26):

> I pray also for those who will believe in me through
> their message, that all of them may be one, Father, just as
> you are in me and I am in you. May they also be in us
> so that the world may believe that you have sent me. I
> have given them the glory that you gave me, that they
> may be one as we are one: I in them and you in me.
> May they be brought to complete unity to let the world
> know that you sent me and have loved them even as you
> have loved me. Father, I want those you have given me
> to be with me where I am, and to see my glory, the
> glory you have given me because you loved me before
> the creation of the world. Righteous Father, though the
> world does not know you, I know you, and they know
> that you have sent me. I have made you known to them,

> and will continue to make you known in order that the
> love you have for me may be in them and that I myself
> may be in them [John 17:20–26, NIV].

It's a symphony of self-giving, of deflecting praise and attention to the other, of spreading the glory around, of serving and
celebrating the goodness of the other rather than of the self.

It is striking in this prayer how the boundaries between
the divine persons are so very permeable. They exist, literally,
"in" each other. It is not even correct to say merely that the
Son is in the Father; this would be logical to our minds, but
it is not what Jesus says. The Son is in the Father and the
Father is in the Son and the disciples are in both. There are
no hard and fast boundary lines between Father, Son, and disciples; love appears to have dissolved them—*and this is precisely the goal.* The German theologian Jürgen Moltmann
refers to the "intimate indwelling
and complete interpenetration of
the persons [of the Trinity] in one
another."[6] Jesus seems to be praying that this kind of love, *a love
that can dissolve all kinds of boundaries and divisions,* will complete
its work on those human beings
in whom it has already begun—
that is, in his disciples—and will
eventually spread to others in the
world who will be drawn into the
community of faith. In the end,
the goal is a cosmic and sublime
unity that emerges when love dis-

> *There are no
> hard and fast
> boundary lines
> between Father,
> Son, and disciples;
> love appears to
> have dissolved
> them—and this is
> precisely the goal.*

solves interpersonal boundaries so that all divine and human
persons will spiritually be one.[7] This is the kind of oneness of

the triune God, and human beings are invited to participate in it through faith. It seems to be the very goal of God in the world and, we know it by faith as the coming shape of the human future, when all the awkwardness, difficulty, and limits of our relationships with each other will be overcome at last.

GOD'S NATURE, HUMAN NATURE

Since we are created in the image of this triune God, that must mean that we are fundamentally created for relationship. In Chapter Two, I suggested that we can perhaps even see traces of that three-in-oneness and one-in-threeness in terms of the internal makeup of the individual self. It is even easier here to claim that any creature made in the image of such a God must be deeply and intrinsically relational. We must resemble God in this core attribute of his being. In his prayer in John 17, Jesus seems to be willing and praying and yearning for the disciples to move into a fuller and fuller experience of that boundary-dissolving interpersonal unity that God enjoys as Father, Son, and Spirit. We are made for relationships of joyful intimacy and interpersonal communion. When we as Christians follow Jesus, we get drafted into that very kind of relationship as it exists within the personhood of God. This is the message of one of the most sublime portions of Scripture, and it resonates profoundly with our other discussions of the inherent human need for relationships along life's journey.

When we catch even the barest glimpse of the level of loving relationship that we see modeled in the triune God, we are reminded in a quite poignant way of how far short we fall. There is something within us that yearns very, very deeply for an end to our alienation from other people. Many of us would give our lives to create, maintain, or preserve even a single relationship of such intimacy. It is what we were made for; it constitutes us as persons; it is powerful enough to build our very identity on.

But given the fact that every human being with whom we seek such a relationship is just as finite, bounded, and limited as we are, if we confine our quest for identity-defining interpersonal communion to other human beings, we will end up deeply disappointed. This is why the Christian tradition has always said that the only relationship that is ultimately secure, the only relationship that is fully trustworthy, the only relationship in which one can fully invest all of one's identity, is a relationship with God.

Likewise, if we bear the image of a God who is triune, this must mean that one of our core tasks in our journey as human beings is to live in redeemed and whole relationships ourselves and to work for such relationships in every corner of the world. The church is designed to be the community that a self-giving, joyfully loving, intrinsically relational God assembles so that we can participate in this sublime divine experience of interpersonal love. This is what we are called to strive for. Whether in our most intimate family relationships or in the church itself as an organization or in our communities and societies or the global human family, we are called to be emissaries of healing and wholeness in relationships. This difficult yet joyful struggle for the healing of alienated relationships—between God and people, among people, and even between people and the nonhuman created order—lies at the heart of the mission of God's people, of the church. Such healing is one way of understanding the meaning of salvation. It comes pretty close to being an excellent definition of the kingdom of God.

But of course, that whole quest for healing assumes that something is not well. Any talk of alienation means that someone is not getting along with someone else. Any talk of salvation assumes that someone needs to be saved. And any mention of the kingdom or reign of God needing to come means that it has not yet come. We cannot defer any longer a discussion of what has gone so wrong with human nature that we need healing, reconciliation, salvation, and the kingdom. In the next chapter, we turn to a consideration of the question of human sin.

4

Am I a "Sinner"?

Only a fool could deny the fact of sin, though
we may choose to call it by another name.
—GERALD VANN

Despite our creation in the image of God, we human
beings are not extravagantly wonderful much of the
time. In fact, we're often unimaginably terrible. We
know exactly what we are supposed to do and not do, yet we
violate our own principles. We fall in love with cars and
houses and out of love with our own children and spouses.
We are so internally torn up that we can't even sleep at night,
so divided in spirit that we don't know who we are. We experience a kind of cosmic loneliness, estranged from the God
who made us. And that doesn't even begin to take in the
enormous terrors of genocide, massacre, war, violence, and
every other awful thing that human beings do to one another
(not to mention the earth and its creatures).

In asking if I'm a "sinner," the quotation marks signal
the contested nature of the term in our day. It seems so
Hester Prynne with her scarlet *A,* so Jonathan Edwards with
his sinners dangling over the fires of hell—in short, so very
old-fashioned. How can I accept such a label for myself?

Instead, I want to run as quickly as I can in the other direction: No, I'm not a sinner; I'm doing the best that I can. No, I'm not a sinner; you should see the other guy at work and what he does. No, I'm not a sinner; I go to church sometimes. No, I'm not a sinner; I make good choices most of the time. No, I'm not a sinner; I do more good than bad.

Although those responses may all be true as far as they go, they don't change the fact: You and I and all of us are definitely sinners. In fact, acknowledging that we are sinners is a key step in the journey toward wholeness. Trying to deny what is bad about ourselves involves constant self-deception and is bound to fail, because the truth will ultimately surface. Such denial also involves us in a constant effort to improve those around us, which is bound to fail as well. But when we own up to the sin in ourselves and others and when we hold it in tension with the goodness and possibility for grandeur, we are on to something. As the philosopher Jean Bethke Elshtain has said, reflecting the wisdom of the Christian tradition, it is both our *dignity* and our *depravity* that characterize our humanity.[1] We must understand both elements as fully as possible.

> *Truth, however unpleasant, is better than illusion. At least we know what we are dealing with.*

So that is what we will try to do in this chapter, at least as far as the depravity part goes. We will explore five dimensions, or five elements, of human sinfulness. In the end, you may well conclude that our human situation is worse than you even thought it was. You may wonder how creatures with so many problems can do anything but crash and burn. But perhaps you will also find that it is a relief to know the truth about yourself and others and the human condition; for truth, however unpleasant, is better than illusion. At least we know what we are dealing with.

THE YEARNING OF CREATION

In the summer of 2004, my family and I went to Gulf Shores, Alabama, for several days at the beach. On our third day there, we read in the local paper about a ten-year-old boy who reported having been bitten by a shark while wading in thigh-deep water quite near the shore. Tendons in his leg were severed, and there were other cuts and bruises, but it would have been a whole lot worse if the boy's grandfather had not wrestled him out of the shark's jaws. Accompanying the newspaper story was a picture of the boy in his hospital bed.

The same story had a quote from the mayor of Gulf Shores saying that his office could not confirm the shark attack. No lifeguards had seen the shark, according to the mayor. Despite the severed tendons in the boy's leg, not to mention what both the boy and his family said they had witnessed, the mayor insisted that the shark attack could not be confirmed.

The story definitely changed the way we spent our time on the beach. For the next two days, we were a lot more careful than we had been. Good thing, too, because one morning the water was cleared after the sighting of a black-finned creature about twenty feet from shore, swimming parallel with it. The next day, my wife saw a similar creature. Though the shark did not officially exist, according to the mayor of Gulf Shores, it certainly did seem to be swimming in waters that no longer looked like a good place for us to be.

There are some striking elements in this story. An average family drives many hours to spend a few days wading at the beach, only to find that an unwanted visitor with sharp teeth seems to have the very same vacation plans. The beach seems like such an idyllic place, and yet it offers numerous dangers to human life, and being eaten by a shark ranks right up there. So fear comes to taint an experience of joyful release from everyday tasks. Also striking is the way that the local officials deny the obvious. It is just as obvious why they did—tourism, money, the financial interests of this beach community. In a time of economic slowdown, the last thing the mayor wants is a confirmed shark sighting, even when that shark takes a bite out of a tourist.

When my family and I found ourselves at the beach, kept out of the water by the sharks cruising just offshore, it reminded us that the world is far from safe or predictable—or even close to perfect. We come into the world as it is—full of suffering, longing, decay, imperfection, chaos, and much worse. We didn't create it, but we not only have to live in it but are also an integral part of it. This sense of being stuck in situations that are wrong but that are not of our making is a common experience for human beings, isn't it? How many times have you thought, I didn't create the mess, but now I have to deal with the consequences?

It is easy to see the way the world is broken and imperfect in the toxic situations that human beings create for themselves and leave behind for others to deal with. Living in the South, as I do, I think about how I didn't create the racial injustices and antagonisms that still exist here, but I still have to deal with their legacy in a thousand different ways. The soldier on the battlefield didn't create the war that led him there, but he still must deal with enemies he doesn't even know who are seeking to disembowel him. Children who are born into abusive families didn't create the abuse in which they are enmeshed, but they still must deal with its impact.

There is something amiss in the world of nature as well and in humans' relationship with it. Beast eats beast in an endless cycle of death. Hornets attack innocent homeowners just trying to cut their lawns. Tornados form and wipe out city blocks; tsunamis form and wipe out whole towns. And children get bitten by sharks. We are simultaneously deeply impressed by the order and grandeur of creation and very much aware that something is deeply disordered there too. It would be nice to have the order without the disorder, the grandeur without the danger, but this does not seem to be an option open to us, at least not yet or not here.
As the Apostle Paul said:

> For the creation waits with eager longing for the
> revealing of the children of God; for the creation was
> subjected to futility, not of its own will but by the will
> of the one who subjected it, in hope that the creation
> itself will be set free from its bondage to decay and will
> obtain the freedom of the glory of the children of God.
> We know that the whole creation has been groaning in
> labor pains until now; and not only the creation, but we
> ourselves, who have the first fruits of the Spirit, groan
> inwardly while we wait for adoption, the redemption
> of our bodies [Romans 8:19–23].

This passage has some pretty distressing images: "the creation waits with eager longing" for the time when its "subjection to futility" and its "bondage to decay" and its "groaning in labor pains" will finally end. In a section that concerns the redemption of human beings saved by Jesus Christ, he brings all of creation into the scenario—just like us, says Paul, creation is a broken thing needing redemption and waiting eagerly for it.

We are all sinners because we are enmeshed in a flawed creation that we cannot escape, flights to the moon notwithstanding. Like a swimmer in the ocean, with all its dangers, we are endangered. Or to use an environmental analogy—the forest is polluted; we are in the forest; therefore, we are polluted too. In either case, there is nowhere we can go to escape.

> *We are all sinners because we are enmeshed in a flawed creation that we cannot escape, flights to the moon notwithstanding.*

In Christian thought, this situation is called "fallenness." Drawn especially from Saint Augustine's reading of the Bible (especially the Genesis stories), the Western Christian tradition has concluded that sin is not just wrong individual choices but generally characteristic of a world that has been pervasively damaged. The classic Christian account of how this has happened is that Adam and Eve sinned, they fell from their perfect state as created by God, and their acts introduced a permanent futility, groaning, enslavement, and decay into not just the human experience but the entire created order. The result of this fallenness is the disorder, distortion, and disruption of God's good design for the world. Fallenness did not erase all traces of order, goodness, and grandeur, but it has affected every aspect of the world, including human nature.

This concept helps sharpen our understanding of human sinfulness quite a bit. It's not just that some people make bad choices and we should try to be good people and thus avoid doing that. It's that human nature itself, in all of its God-given dignity and goodness, has been bent, corrupted, and disordered and that brokenness is reflected in the world. The concept of original sin, so often rejected, disputed, or simply misunderstood in different strands of Christian (and non–Christian) thought, is basically a way of saying that no human being can escape the taint and the effects of the Fall, and in each generation (and every life), we recapitulate the story of the Fall by our own choices. Our fallenness inclines us toward sin, as individuals and communities, and it also enmeshes all of us in a distorted and disrupted social and natural world. And our fallenness never goes away. Sin is over us, on us, in us, and around us. It is a permanent aspect of the human condition, a kind of "ancestral shadow" from which we never can fully emerge.[2]

There is a house on my street right now that has been abandoned by its bankrupt owners. Neither they nor anyone else is living there, and no one is regularly taking care of the place. A tree fell during a storm and lay there for weeks, its leaves slowly browning. The uncut grass is often knee-high. The vines and shrubs are climbing the house. The back deck and parts of the inside of the house are literally collapsing. We—each of us, and our world—are like this house, which has fallen (or is always falling) into decay and disrepair. It's a dynamic process, a metaphor of motion. When the Fall occurred, the world fell with a great crash, "and great was its fall," as Jesus said in Matthew 7:27. We are like a once-beautiful house that stands in partial ruins. That is not the end of the story, and it wasn't the beginning, but it is a part of the story and thus an important part of our journey. Am I a sinner? Yes, absolutely, in the sense that I am fallen, and I live in a fallen world. In rediscovering this tragic fact each day, I groan in my spirit, like the earth itself.

OF BROKEN RELATIONSHIPS

"When Judas, his betrayer, saw that Jesus was condemned, he repented and brought back the thirty pieces of silver to the chief priests and the elders. He said, 'I have sinned by betraying innocent blood.' But they said, 'What is that to us? See to it yourself.' Throwing down the pieces of silver in the temple, he departed; and he went and hanged himself" (Matthew 27:3–5).

Is there a more wretched figure than Judas anywhere in the Bible? Here is a man who has spent three years walking and talking with Jesus, just like the other apostles, privileged beyond measure to be in Jesus' inner circle. There were only twelve, after all, and he was one of them. But for some reason he betrayed his Master. No one knows exactly why Judas acted as he did—at least in terms of his own reasons for acting—but we do know that he repented bitterly of his sin and "saw to it himself" by ending his own life.

> *Things can go wrong in a myriad of ways, whereas success in life's journey is like a single narrow path that must be found and kept to.*

In his great novel *Anna Karenina,* Leo Tolstoy wrote, "All happy families resemble one another, but each unhappy family is unhappy in its own way." Aristotle said something similar: "Men are bad in countless ways, but good in only one."[3]

One can quibble with both of these claims, but there is certainly some truth to the idea that getting it right is a whole lot more difficult than getting it wrong. Things can go wrong in a myriad of ways, whereas success in life's journey is like a single narrow path that must be found and kept to. And that is just as true for our relationships as it is for any other aspect of human life. However reluctant we might be to admit it, a second irrefutable piece of evidence of our sinfulness is the fragility of our relationships. We spent all of Chapter Three talking about how human beings are intrinsically relational creatures, how that quality is wired into our very nature as made in God's image, and how we flourish when our relationships flourish.

But often they do not flourish. It seems that we are more adept at getting our relationships wrong than at getting them right. This critical dimension of our very personhood as made in God's image is critically brittle. And so we spend much of our time trying to recover from broken relationships, heal damaged ones, and maintain healthy ones.

In my e-mail address book is the name of an old friend from whom I am estranged. We became estranged several years ago after he was forced out of a church job that I helped him get. Our friendship never quite recovered. It was a combination of factors: his hurt feelings during the problems at church, a failure on my part to follow up adequately, and a fear (probably on both sides) of initiating a conversation that might be painful (but might also lead to reconciliation). Finally, he moved away. And so his name continues to sit in my address book, waiting for the day when I will be brave enough to send him an e-mail.

Friendships are especially fragile because they are voluntary relationships that require mutual enjoyment and satisfaction for them to continue happily. Compared to family relationships, it is easier to walk away from a friendship. But that does not diminish the pain when a friendship is betrayed, as in the case of Judas, or damaged and never healed, as in the case of my estranged friend, or frittered away, as is so often the case. One proof that I am a sinner, and that all of us are sinners, is my awareness of the fragility of my friendships and the number of friends I have lost along the way.

Marriage may be the ultimate test case of sin-as-broken-relationships because it is in many ways the ultimate human relationship. One does not have to be a marriage and family counselor to know something about the fragility of this particular relationship. As a minister and professor who spends a lot of time counseling happy young engaged couples and troubled married couples, this particular aspect of human relationships is pretty familiar to me. It is more than tempting to believe that the formula is ironclad: smitten engaged couple + twenty years = miserable married couple.

In this case, I think that Tolstoy is right in suggesting that all happy couples are similar, whereas unhappiness in marriage takes many forms. Certainly it is true that married couples exhibit a wide range of marital styles, but at the heart of most happy contemporary marriages is a loving, faithful, mutually satisfying sexual friendship. Perhaps in other eras and other contexts this particular set of attributes was not viewed as necessary, but today, in our culture, all are important, at least to the overwhelming majority of people.

But look at how difficult it is for fallen, sinful human beings to accomplish what is indicated by the words *loving, faithful, mutually satisfying sexual friendship.* Successful marriage requires two people who have the basic capacity to function as loving, faithful, sexual friends. If either one of the two lacks essential competencies in any of these dimensions, the relationship will fail. Many people lack the willingness or ability to love, to maintain exclusive commitments, to offer and receive sexual fulfillment, or to preserve a friendship. Some people start off with full capacities in each area but then lose one or another of them due to any number of causes, large and small—substance abuse, neglect, ill health, bad choices, anger, lack of forgiveness. Some people make a single bad choice—such as a thoughtless sexual affair—that destroys a relationship that was otherwise good. Some people become pathological, turning against the one they care about most in a poisonous hatefulness that annihilates the relationship altogether.

Ultimately, love is the virtue required for any relationship to flourish, whether with those closest at hand or those who are less intimate. But love itself reveals the pathetic internal contradictions within the human soul, for love is both central to our lives and relationships and all too fragile and easily obstructed. We know that we need to love but lack the ability to do it; we know the fuel that makes relationships go but can't quite muster enough of it. And so for lack of love our relationships struggle and sometimes die.

Am I a sinner? Yes, absolutely, because in a fallen world, my most important relationships are fragile, and I am often the one at fault for destroying rather than preserving or enhancing them. Who among us can look at his or her own life's battlefield, strewn with the casualties of a lifetime's worth of broken or abandoned relationships, and deny that there is something very deeply and intrinsically wrong?

OF MORAL RULES AND THEIR VIOLATION

The Apostle Paul was especially forthcoming about the way he wrestled with his sinful nature:

> For we know that the law is spiritual; but I am of the
> flesh, sold into slavery under sin. I do not understand my
> own actions. For I do not do what I want, but I do the

> very thing I hate. Now if I do what I do not want, I
> agree that the law is good. But in fact it is no longer
> I that do it, but sin that dwells within me. For I know
> that nothing good dwells within me, that is, in my flesh.
> I can will what is right, but I cannot do it. For I do not
> do the good I want, but the evil I do not want is what
> I do. Now if I do what I do not want, it is no longer
> I that do it, but sin that dwells within me [Romans
> 7:14–20].

If sin is understood as the violation of important moral
rules, most of us would acknowledge that this is something
we have certainly done. Indeed, many people locate their entire understanding of sin right here, as the violation of moral
rules, and few honest people would claim that they have always upheld them. But the issue of moral rules and our relation to them is surprisingly complex. There is, for example,
the very question of how we know such rules exist. Paul's
source of knowledge of moral rules had been the Torah,
Jewish Law. In the Jewish worldview, God has established the
moral rules that govern the universe and that are recorded in
sacred Scripture, Israel stands in a covenant relationship with
God that obligates each Jew to keep these rules, and their
authority is reinforced by ongoing worship and study practices. Faithful Jews seek to internalize the Law and make it
the governing force of their life and behavior, not just out of
obligation but out of love for God and gratitude for his moral
direction. The psalmist says, "I rejoice at your word like one
who finds great spoil. I hate and abhor falsehood, but I love
your law. Seven times a day do I praise you for your righteous
ordinances" (Psalm 119:163).

Many Christians carry essentially the same concept of
the nature and authority of moral rules. They come from
God himself, are revealed in the Bible, are binding on the

believer and to some extent on all humanity, are reinforced by church and family, and are to be internalized in our consciences on the basis of love for God.

In this view, sin is the violation of authoritative moral rules, laws, or commands. The question is not whether I know what I am supposed to do (or not do) but whether I do what I know I must—and refrain from doing what I know I must not do. The role of the moral self is thus to accept the authority and truthfulness of this law or rule imposed from outside and eventually to internalize it so that it becomes my own standard of behavior, enforced by personal conscience. In the biblical traditions, the original source of this morality is God, the divine Commander, who carries the authority both to compel moral obedience and to judge disobedience.

Many modern people dislike any suggestion that the morality by which people live has been imposed on them from outside of themselves. Sigmund Freud reduced the notion to a projection of our infantile sense of powerlessness in the face of our rule-making and rule-enforcing parents. Immanuel Kant believed that moral rules must be imposed on the self by the self—and on the basis of reason, not divine revelation. Sociologists and anthropologists often point to the role of our communities in shaping our understanding of moral rules. Many today would say that they have rejected belief in God—or belief that the Bible is the revealed Word of God—and govern themselves based on the dictates of their own conscience or perhaps the legal or cultural standards of their communities.

But even if the authority for moral rules shifts from God or sacred text to reason, community, or conscience, *still we must admit that we violate the moral rules that we ourselves accept as authoritative.* We violate *our own* principles, our own conscience, our own community standards, our own reason.

Shifting the source and authority for moral rules doesn't solve the problem that we break rules.

If sin is violation of moral rules, it takes a variety of forms. Sometimes, if we simply do not know what the relevant moral rules are, we violate them unwittingly. Perhaps this is due to deficient moral training or immaturity on our part, or a particularly complex moral issue confronts us and we do not meet the challenge successfully. In a delightful phrase, the Roman Catholic tradition calls this "invincible ignorance," which means that the sinner is not *fully* responsible for the act, having had no way of overcoming ignorance about it.

More often, though, we do know that an act is wrong, but we do it anyway. Sometimes, as parents well know, we (like the children we once were) break rules due to sheer orneriness, rebelliousness, or willfulness. Many observers of human nature have remarked at this rule-breaking streak in human nature—establish a rule or law, and somebody will come to the fore very quickly to break it because, like Mount Everest, it's there.

It is striking, though, that most of us do not baldly violate moral rules whose authority and relevance we accept. We don't just say, "I know adultery is wrong, but I want to do it anyway." Instead, part of sinful human nature is our seemingly endless capacity to rationalize our wrong actions, to claim that the rules don't apply to us, to evade responsibility, to shift blame, to deceive ourselves, or to relabel our acts with new language. As the theologian Wendy Farley writes, "Deception may be the most ubiquitous feature of sin."[4] Thus the Nazis, as they murdered millions, rationalized their actions as necessary for national defense and "racial purity," claimed that normal laws of war were not relevant in the midst of their apocalyptic struggle for survival, blamed their victims, and lied to themselves about their deeds by relabeling mass murder as "euthanasia" or "special treatment." When Nazi perpetrators were captured and tried, most shifted blame so as not to have to bear full responsibility. The courts were not convinced that "I was just following orders" was a viable defense, and I agree. But how often do we resort to the same kind of move when faced with our own sins?

Paul speaks to yet another dimension of sin as rule breaking in the passage quoted from Romans 7. He is conscious of a split within himself. There is a tear in his spirit. He knows what is right, but there is another force within him that threatens to prevail. His language here is very interesting. The "I" shifts—"I do not understand what 'I' do. It is no longer 'I myself' who do it but sin living 'in me.'" He is saying that there is a force inside the flesh, inside me, that blocks the real me from doing right, from carrying out my *own* intentions. This is the case even though he has a relationship with Jesus Christ and access to God's Spirit.

Paul then tries another formulation. In my "inner being," he says, I delight in God's law, but there is another "law" at work in the "members" of my body. It's a war, a war between two aspects of myself, two "laws" both resident within me, a civil war tearing me apart. And so Paul concludes with the pitiable lament: "What a wretched man I am! Who shall rescue me from this body of death?" And his answer? "Thanks be to God—through Jesus Christ our Lord" (Romans 7:24–25).

If this is sin as rule breaking, it has an entirely new dimension to it, because the rule breaker is caught up in the grip of a powerful countervailing force within his own self. Perhaps the best way to describe this is that we break rules because we are *enslaved to sin*. We will return to this issue in the next chapter, but what is introduced here is the question of whether we really are as free as we think we are to avoid sinful acts. Paul seems to be saying that even the committed Christian can be enslaved to patterns of sin, despite serious efforts to the contrary, efforts that are aided by God's Spirit. If this enslavement to sin can happen to someone struggling energetically against it, what must it be like for the person who does not struggle but simply succumbs? Surely such a person must be completely in the grip of sin, like a fly in a spider's web. If sin has spun its web around us, the good news, if there is any, is that we can hardly be viewed as fully responsible for our acts, because responsibility correlates with freedom. If we are not free, however, the bad news is that sin is in a sense unavoidable. But can it really be that we are truly lacking in any freedom not to sin? The great Christian thinker, Augustine of Hippo, denied it, saying, "No one sins by acts he cannot avoid."[5] Yet Augustine himself wrote quite acutely on the experience of enslavement to sin. Even though it doesn't exhaust our understanding of sin, this concept of our enslavement to sin—and thus the surprising limits of our cherished moral freedom—is a topic we will take up in the next chapter.

OF MISDIRECTED LOVE

It was Augustine who first articulated the key insight that sin is misdirected love.[6] Deeply influenced by the Greek philosophical tradition, Augustine noticed the strong emphasis in that tradition on the relentless human quest for happiness. Aristotle, for example, opened his ethics lectures by claiming that "every action and pursuit is considered to aim at some good," and this good is "happiness," understood as "living well or doing well."[7] We do what we do because we believe that it will make us happy one way or another. So the philosophical task is to help people figure out what true happiness consists of and how best to get there. This was Aristotle's understanding of the ultimate destination in life's journey.

Augustine deepened this analysis and drew it together with more explicitly Christian thinking by claiming that everything we do is an expression of some kind of love. We love objects, like cars and computers, and the pleasures they bring us. We love people, beginning with ourselves. Some of us love God or at least religion. Thus our actions both reflect and advance our loves. We do what we love, and our actions tend to deepen our love for whatever that love is directed toward, whether it is golf or fine dining or the New York Jets.

One of the most devilishly subtle forms of sin is misdirected or disordered love. We love self too much and others too little. We love things too much and people too little. We love people but we love them selfishly, for how they please us. We love God but mainly for what we think God can do for us, rather than for what God has already done for us or for what we can do for God.

What makes this kind of sin so formidable a problem is that most of the things we love are lovely in their own way. It is not wrong to love most of the things we love. The affection we feel for a good book, a fine meal, a charming painting, or a good time is not wrong or evil. But if we love any of these more than a person, or if we love any person more than God, our loves are disordered. This is why Scripture directs us to love God most (and first) and to love our neighbors as ourselves. This idea of a kind of hierarchy of love is sometimes troubling for faithful Christians, as we find ourselves juggling the priority of the various loves in our lives. If mishandled, it can be the source of real tension and some misguided behavior, such as the pastor who so loves God that he completely neglects his wife and children or the wife who loves her children so much that she neglects her husband.

But still, we can see the truth of this graded hierarchy of loves if we just think about it a little bit. Consider what we would think of a man who rushed into his burning home to retrieve his television and DVD collection while leaving his children to burn to death. Or think of a person who voluntarily moved across the country to follow a job he enjoyed, even though it meant leaving his wife and children behind indefinitely. (Actually, many people do this, some of them because, sadly, they have little choice in the matter if they want to survive.) All loves are not created equal. Some are of higher significance than others and must be treated as such.

I have a vivid memory of some relatives that my family and I used to visit when I was a kid. This family was possession-rich but happiness-poor. Every time we saw these relatives, they had a new car, nicer clothes, and the newest gadgets. Our old beat-up stuff always looked bad by comparison. But they were not happy. It seemed to us that they bought stuff in an attempt to find happiness but that such happiness could be acquired only through more love, not more toys. Although I would have been pleased to drive to family vacations in a decent-looking car that had air conditioning, I ended up soberly grateful each summer in our trusty old clunker that I had the family I did.

Moral rules are not quite the right category for dealing with this form of sin. We can see this when we consider the story of the rich young man, from Matthew 19.

> Then someone came to him and said, "Teacher, what good deed must I do to have eternal life?" And he said

to him, "Why do you ask me about what is good?
There is only one who is good. If you wish to enter
into life, keep the commandments." He said to him,
"Which ones?" And Jesus said, "You shall not murder;
You shall not commit adultery; You shall not steal; You
shall not bear false witness; Honor your father and
mother; also, you shall love your neighbor as yourself."
The young man said to him, "I have kept all these; what
do I still lack?" Jesus said to him, "If you wish to be
perfect, go, sell your possessions, and give the money
to the poor, and you will have treasure in heaven; then
come, follow me." When the young man heard this
word, he went away grieving, for he had many possessions. Then Jesus said to his disciples, "Truly I tell you,
it will be hard for a rich person to enter the kingdom
of heaven" [Matthew 19:16–23].

This young man seems to be a conventionally but seriously
pious Jewish man. He apparently cannot be charged with
breaking any of the Ten Commandments; Jesus goes through
six of them, one by one, and the man has broken none of
them. So his is not the sin of rule violation. But he knows
that something is missing, and Jesus pinpoints it with acuity:
he loves his stuff too much, as you can see when Jesus invites
him to sell everything, give to the poor, and join his traveling
band of disciples. The man went away grieving, the story tells
us, because he had many possessions. In a contest between the
love he had for those possessions and the love for God-in-
Christ to which he was invited, he chose his possessions. Thus
it is excruciatingly difficult, as Jesus says, to get a rich man
through the needle's eye and into heaven—not because possessions are evil but because they elicit our love, and our love
can only be directed in so many places before it is exhausted.
The advantage the impoverished person has in this regard is

not inconsiderable. Lacking possessions to love, one's heart is more readily available to extend love to God.

In his *Confessions,* Augustine discusses his discovery of the disordered loves in his own life. He tells the story of the death of one of his dearest friends when both were young men. His depiction of the inconsolable grief he experiences in losing his friend is one of the most insightful in all of literature. Reflecting on this experience, Augustine concludes that his problem was not that he loved his friend so much but that he did not love him *in God*. He was not able to think of his friend in terms of the friend's relationship with God, and thus the friend's joyful eternal destiny of life with God did not bring Augustine any kind of consolation. Instead, Augustine was obsessed with what his friend's death cost *him,* now left behind to go on alone. Reflecting later on this situation as a mature Christian, Augustine concluded that only when love for God lies at the center and pinnacle of all of our other loves can these other loves be rightly ordered.

SIN AS ALIENATION FROM GOD

> Fools say in their hearts, "There is no God."
> They are corrupt, they do abominable deeds;
> there is no one who does good.
> The LORD looks down from heaven on
>   humankind
> to see if there are any who are wise,
> who seek after God.
> They have all gone astray, they are all alike perverse;
> there is no one who does good,
> no, not one [Psalm 14:1–3].

The Bible is stubborn in its affirmation that rejecting God is both the ultimate sin and the foundation of other sins. Human beings are sinners because we turn our backs on the God who made us, who sustains our lives, who gives us every good gift, who reveals his moral will to us, who watches our every deed, who has provided for our eternal salvation, and who is the judge of the living and the dead.

Rejecting such a God is, in biblical terms, simply a denial of reality. There was no argument about the existence of God within the life of the biblical peoples, but instead the argument had to do with the best way to serve and honor him. To them, as to those of us who believe in God, to deny God is to deny reality, to deny the very source of our own existence, to deny this source proper gratitude, and to invite divine judgment and wrath.

To deny God is also to deny ourselves access to moral truth. This is the theme of the passage from Psalm 14, and it is echoed in both the Old and the New Testament. Fools say there is no God, and not coincidentally, they are corrupt and do abominable deeds. Left to their own devices, rebelling against God and his Law, fools grow increasingly corrupt and their acts increasingly vile. It is as if God is the sun that illuminates the landscape of the moral life; when the sun is eclipsed, the land is dark, and the people are left to wander around without direction or sight. The end result is sheer folly.[8]

Paul makes much the same argument in Romans 1–2. There he claims that even those who have never heard of the God of Israel had plenty of access to evidence concerning his will and character through what was plainly revealed to them, both in the world and in their own consciences. But the people of the pagan world rejected the knowledge that was available to them, and so the lights went out—"their sense-less minds were darkened" (Romans 1:21). They "exchanged the truth of God for a lie" (1:25), both in worship and in morality, and thus tumbled over a cliff into moral and spiritual ruin. Their life's journey ended not in wholeness but in destruction.

As influenced by Paul, the Christian tradition made a decisive break with Judaism precisely on the interpretation of Psalm 14 and the issues it raises. Paul quoted it in Romans 3 (see verses 10–12) to make the case that indeed, "all have sinned and fall short of the glory of God" (3:23). There is no righteous person, not a single one, as, read literally, Psalm 14 says; we have all gone astray, we are all perverse, we have all corrupted our ways, and not one of us does good. For Paul, this was decisive evidence that both Jews and non-Jews alike need the salvation available in Jesus Christ. This salvation not only means forgiveness of our many sins but also the beginnings of empowerment to a new kind of moral living. For believers, at least, the sun will begin to shine again; the moral landscape will be illuminated, through Jesus Christ, the light of the world, by the power of the Holy Spirit.

> *For believers, at least, the sun will begin to shine again; the moral landscape will be illuminated, through Jesus Christ, the light of the world, by the power of the Holy Spirit.*

The Jewish tradition didn't read Psalm 14 that way. It saw, and continues to see, the human family as consisting of some who reject God and his ways and others who do not. We do not need to be rescued from some kind of pervasive original sin that covers us all but instead need to love God, learn his ways, and do right. There is a good instinct and an evil instinct that compete within all of us, and the good can prevail if we make the right choices. Thus to the Jewish tradition, the question "Am I a sinner?" is best answered, "If I make sinful choices, yes." But for the classic Christian tradition, the answer is an unequivocal yes. The best of us are sinners, even those who have been saved by Jesus Christ and have embarked on a Spirit-empowered life. As Augustine put it, "However much you may advance in the love of God and of your neighbor, and in true piety, do not imagine as long as you are in this life, that you are without sin."9

This is a darker vision of the human condition and certainly an arguable one. But when we review the forms of sin we have considered in this chapter, such Augustinian pessimism makes more sense. We are sinners because we are fallen, and we live in a groaning, fallen world, whose disorder affects all that we are and do. We are sinners because we break relationships (and hearts), even those that are dearest to us. We are sinners because we violate moral rules that we ourselves often heartily believe in, even becoming enslaved to patterns of sin. We are sinners because our loves are misdirected and disordered. We are sinners either because we reject the God who made us and his ways or because we live as functional atheists regardless of our profession of faith. Thus we rush around as if in a dark room, harming ourselves and everyone unfortunate enough to get in our way.

There is certainly hope in the Christian faith. The fact that we are sinners is not the last word to be said about us. Our journey need not end on that sad note. Human beings are God's damaged image-bearers, dignified *and* depraved *and* being redeemed, in a creation that itself shall one day be fully redeemed. That's the whole story. Each part is important.

5

Am I Really Free?

In divine and spiritual things we have no free will.
—MARTIN LUTHER

We have to believe in free will. We've got no choice.
—ISAAC BASHEVIS SINGER

I used to love to eat some really-bad-for-you but delicious processed foods—anything with a creamy filling is a real temptation. In recent years, though, as I have watched nature take its course and begun fighting the battle of the bulge, I have sworn off such treats. I never buy them at the grocery store, and I certainly never buy them if someone else is with me.

But a strange thing has happened. When I go out to fill up my car at the gas station just down the road from my house, I occasionally succumb to temptation and buy myself one of those creamy treats. After a while, I noticed that I was getting a little sugar fix every time I went to the gas station. Then I realized that I was finding a way to stop at the gas station and get a treat whenever I was running an errand of any kind.

On days when I was feeling particularly resolute about diet and fitness, I would still go to the gas station but would get a "lower-calorie" treat of some kind rather than the big gooey one I liked best. I felt more virtuous, but I still got my treat. I was having my cake and eating it, too—literally.

Eventually, I realized that over time I had conditioned myself to a certain pattern of action, as if an internal tape clicked on whenever I started the engine of my car: *David Gushee, whenever you go out on an errand you will stop at a gas station and spend money on a treat.* Like a robot, I did this every time, until I noticed it. Even after I noticed it and tried to stop, I felt what sometimes seemed like an irresistible compulsion to do it anyway. I could actually watch myself going through these same dynamics each time: I'd get in the car to run an errand, feel a compulsion to stop at the gas station, struggle with what treat to buy, buy the treat anyway, and eat it with a concurrent sense of pleasure (*how gooey and wonderful!*) and guilt (*you undisciplined porker!*).

Recognizing this pattern raised a fundamental question in my mind—was I, am I, truly free *not to stop* at the gas station and drift over to the Twinkies aisle? Are you free to stop doing something that you routinely do in your life? To start doing something you believe you should do? More broadly, are we free to make what we usually call "choices"? Most of us think we are free, but are we really? Are there forces that lie behind or underneath or beyond our decision-making power that actually determine our behavior? Can it be that when we are making what we think of as a free

> *Can it be that when we are making what we think of as a free choice among several alternatives, we are not actually making a free choice at all?*

choice among several alternatives, we are not actually making a free choice at all?

The existence and extent of human freedom is a major issue to be considered in any account of human nature. It should be acutely relevant to anyone who has found oneself in the grip of forces that seem beyond one's personal control (as I did)—and yet not entirely. Freedom has everything to do with our quest for wholeness, since it raises questions about who is in charge.

This chapter takes up these questions, looking at perspectives that claim that we are not as free in our choices as we commonly think we are, before moving to a Christian account that preserves at least a limited vision of human moral freedom. This is a critically important issue in understanding human nature and the possibility we have of finding wholeness in our life journey.

GOD DOES IT ALL

In the history of Christian thought, many people have been attracted to the concept that God determines everything that happens on this planet. If it happens, God did it. It's not a big logical leap from the concept to the assumption that God must determine human decisions as well. If that's the case, it seems logical to conclude either that we are not truly free or that we are free but our freedom is a watered-down version unlike anything we normally understand freedom to mean.[1] Either way, though we think we are charting our own course on life's journey, in some way this sense of self-direction is an illusion.

The high-powered vision of God's determination of all events is arrived at, in part, through reading the Bible. A number of stories communicate the idea that God has determined the course of events in a situation, even if the human actors in the story do not know it—or even if they seek to achieve very different ends. A great example is in the story, in Genesis 37–50, of Joseph, the precocious, talented, irritating young Israelite whose older brothers hated him, threw him down an empty well and left him for dead, and finally sold him into slavery. Through a series of extraordinary events, Joseph ends up as prime minister of Egypt and the man who will determine the earthly destiny of the very brothers who hated him. The entire story is told from the perspective that God has directed these events for a particular set of purposes and that no human could thwart God's will. Human beings make their own decisions, but a more powerful hidden will directs events in its own way. As Joseph says in the climactic scene of this grand story, "Even though you intended to do harm to me, God intended it for good" (Genesis 50:20). And what God intends prevails.

The point is even more acutely felt in the series of stories that follow, in the book of Exodus. Joseph is long dead, and the Jews are in bondage under a genocidal Egyptian pharaoh. God calls Moses to serve as Israel's leader and send him to tell Pharaoh to "let my people go" (Exodus 5:1). But Pharaoh just won't do it, even though Egypt suffers under a staggering series of divine judgments that destroy crops, poison water, and kill animals and people. The Bible says directly that God "hardened Pharaoh's heart" (4:21)—and this is why Pharaoh will not yield. And yet Pharaoh is also consistently indicted for his stubborn resistance to God's commands. The end result is the great Exodus of the Jews from Egypt, a decisive event in the history of Israel as told in the Bible. The implication is the same as in the Joseph story: we may think we are making our own decisions, but God is instead directing events—perhaps in some kind of mysterious interaction with our choices, but God is in charge nevertheless, and we are actors in his play.

This perspective can also be deduced logically from certain beliefs about God, deeply held in the Christian tradition, that point to divine direction of all events and diminish human freedom:

1. The Bible tells us that God is all-powerful; he has the complete ability to accomplish whatever he chooses to do (Psalm 115:3, 135:6; Job 42:2; Daniel 4:35; Ephesians 1:11).
2. The Bible also tells us that God is sovereign over the earth and all who dwell on earth; he is the unquestioned ruler of the world he has made (Psalm 10:16, 24; Romans 11:36; and elsewhere).
3. If, however, an event that God has not determined can happen on earth, God is neither all-powerful nor sovereign; his power in that case must be somehow limited, and his rule must be somehow less than total.
4. These claims are not in keeping with Scripture.
5. Therefore, God must determine all events.

There are many who find a vision of life in which God determines everything that happens not just true to the Bible's witness but also immensely comforting in the face of a world full of evil and peril. John Calvin, the sixteenth-century theologian who founded Presbyterianism and who is strongly identified with a high view of God's direction of all events, contrasted the reassuring security of such a stance to what he considered the terror of believing that anything could happen on this planet that falls outside of God's determination:

"Those who ascribe just praise to God's omnipotence doubly benefit thereby. First, power ample enough to do good there is in him in whose possession are heaven and earth, and to whose beck all creatures are so attentive as to put themselves in obedience to him. Secondly, they may safely rest in the protection of him to whose will are subject all the harmful things which, whatever their source, we may fear."[2]

While we may understand and appreciate such a stance, ultimately (at least in its strongest form) it does not satisfy most Christians today. Objections are many, the most cogent of them being the following three:

• God is loving and good, so it is very difficult to accept the idea that God is directly the author or cause of the many outrageously evil events that occur on earth. (The Holocaust may be the most painful single example.) We cannot sustain a doctrine of God's omnipotence at the cost of losing God's goodness. Somehow we must resolve this issue in a way that maintains belief in both attributes of God.

• To attribute all human-caused events and decisions entirely to God rather than to human beings appears to make it impossible to hold people morally accountable for their actions. If we accept this view, it seems to render all the Bible's (and Dad's and Mom's and Teacher's and everyone else's) moral exhortations meaningless. We cannot sustain a doctrine of God's omnipotence at the cost of losing meaningful human moral responsibility.

• Our sense that we have at least a significant range of freedom in our choices cannot be entirely dismissed as an illusion without throwing into doubt the meaningfulness of all our perceptions. We cannot sustain a doctrine of God's omnipotence at the cost of losing the overwhelming evidence of our human perceptions and experiences, in which we face forks in the road of life, must choose, and do choose. The same problem exists at the other end of the intellectual spectrum as we confront those who treat human freedom as an illusion due to other philosophical or scientific perspectives. In both cases, we are forced to throw out the daily evidence of our own choice-making and end up diminishing the meaning of human life as a result.

If we depart from the assumption that God determines the course of all events, we must, as Christians who rely on the Bible, find a way to accommodate these seemingly conflicting contentions about God's sovereign direction of history and human events and God's goodness and the meaningfulness of human choices. The best surviving option, it seems to me, is to say that although God knows in advance all the choices we will make and directly causes some events (including certain events that appear to us to be morally evil—see 1 Samuel 16:15 and 2 Samuel 24), as a basic policy decision he chooses to permit (rather than direct) other events, including most human choices. Think of Adam and Eve, for example, who exercised their freedom wrongly and plunged the human family into sin. It is hard to read Genesis 1–3 to say that God directed that disobedience. But he certainly permitted it. If this is how God works most of the time, we can say that God is both all-powerful and sovereign while also protecting the concept of real human freedom. This is at least one solution to this very difficult dilemma.

In both Scripture and history, we can see a kind of pattern (as in the story of Joseph or of Judas' betrayal of Jesus) in which humans make their choices for their own reasons, but God makes use of these choices in his own way. In this view,

God really is sovereign, and there really is more going on in life than we can perceive from the ebb and flow of daily events, but most human choices are still both free and meaningful.[3] This preserves the significance of the decisions we make in our quest for wholeness in life—as wise or unwise as those decisions may be—while alerting us to the reality of another level of activity beyond our awareness.

THE DEVIL MADE ME DO IT

A quite contrary but related and in some ways remarkably similar idea is the belief that a personal Devil at times takes over our actions and robs us of our freedom to make moral choices. It is easy to laugh off the old saying that "the Devil made me do it," but one does not have to go far into the highways and byways to find people who are convinced that Satan, the Devil, Beelzebub, or whatever you want to call him is alive and well and affecting human decisions.

Belief in evil spirits and a supernatural evil being can be found both within and outside the Christian tradition. Satan himself is mentioned just a few times in the Old Testament, most notably in the book of Job (where he functions as Job's adversary and the one who triggers the whole calamitous series of events that happens to him), but in the New Testament, words translated as "Satan," the "Devil," or "demons" are mentioned more than one hundred forty times. In essence, Satan is treated as a kind of parallel but not equal to God, a supernatural evil being who presides over a court of lesser demonic beings and angels (Matthew 25:41) and devotes his efforts to advancing a kingdom of evil (12:26). Whatever God does and seeks to do on the planet, Satan seeks to block; whatever supernatural resources God can bring to bear to advance his agenda, Satan can muster a parallel but less powerful arsenal on the other side.

Specifically, the New Testament depicts Satan blocking the Gospel message from being heard (Mark 4:15), causing human suffering and illness (Luke 13:15–16; 2 Corinthians 12:7), possessing people's souls or bodies (Matthew 4:24), hatching various schemes, plots, tricks, and traps against Jesus and his followers (Matthew 4:1–11; 2 Corinthians 11:14; 2 Timothy 2:26), sending evil spirits on various missions (Revelation 18:2), using people to tempt or test others, or just tempting them directly, including Jesus himself (Matthew 4:1–11, 16:23), blocking the legitimate plans of Christian missionaries (1 Thessalonians 2:18), and holding the power of death (Hebrews 2:14).

The New Testament offers various depictions and descriptions of the ways Satan controls (or attempts to control) human beings. It begins with his settled determination to oppose God, advance evil, and win as many human beings to his cause as possible. Pursuing the agenda of temptation, misdirection, deception, and trickery that is common among determined but outmatched adversaries (such as insurgents or guerrillas in conflicts all over the world), Satan is described as one who "always prowls around, looking for someone to devour" (1 Peter 5:8). He probes human beings for weaknesses, looking for a "foothold" (Ephesians 4:27) in their spirits. He is especially interested in testing the faith, steadfastness, and moral purpose of believers in Christ in order to snatch people away from Christ their Lord and hinder the work of the church (Luke 22:31; 1 Corinthians 7:5).

Once he gains a foothold, Satan is free to extend his control over ever-larger regions of the person and his or her behavior, unless the person resists. This is sometimes described in the Gospels in the language of demon possession—those most deeply consumed by Satan's power are depicted as being the spiritual residence not just of one demon but of multiple demons (Mark 5:1–20).

In perhaps the most notable examples, Satan is described as "entering into" Judas Iscariot (Matthew 22:3) and as having "filled [the] heart" of Ananias and Sapphira, the couple who attempted to deceive the apostles about a sale of land and were struck dead for having done so (Acts 5:1ff). These people were vulnerable to Satan for their own reasons; Satan was able to penetrate their weakened defenses and make himself at home. They are certainly not the only ones ever to succumb. Jesus describes the world as being like a field full of both good wheat and bad weeds, with the latter the "children of the evil one," sowed by the Devil (Matthew 13:38–39). In his quest for human beings, Satan wins a significant number of victories. His victims end up spiritually and morally destroyed.

Nevertheless, Satan is *never* depicted as irresistible and *never* viewed as more powerful than God. Satan takes control of people's choices only if they open the door to him and do not resist him. In certain lives the demons dance, but it does not have to be this way. The Bible consistently says that Satan is on the prowl, but he can be beaten or at least avoided. "Resist the Devil and he will flee from you" (James 4:7); "Do not give the Devil a foothold" (Ephesians 4:27)— these exhortations would be nonsense if human beings (at least, human beings who believe in Jesus Christ) lack the power to resist Satan's tricks, temptations, and schemes.

Moreover, the New Testament offers many instances and declarations that God's power is greater than Satan's and that God's kingdom will prevail and is prevailing. "Lord, in your name even the demons submit to us!" say the disciples, and Jesus celebrates with them: "I saw Satan fall from heaven like a flash of lightning" (Luke 10:17–18). The timing of this demise of Satan raises one of the New Testament's most difficult questions. Verb tenses matter here: Satan *has been* defeated by the work of Christ (meaning the defeat is in the past); Satan *is being* defeated (the work of defeat is ongoing); "the God of peace *will shortly crush* (the defeat is close to happening) Satan under your feet" (Romans 16:20); Satan will one day be destroyed forever (the defeat is definitely in the future) in the climactic act of cosmic redemption at the end of time (Revelation 20:10).

What it seems to amount to is this: *in light of the superior power of God and the saving work of Christ, Satan need not ever have control of anyone's life.* To the extent that Satan does succeed in devouring souls, it is because he is still at work probing for chinks in our armor—and there are still such weak spots to be found in every one of us. So we can't really say that "the Devil made me do it," if we're implying no choice in the matter. The choice is whether to give the Devil a foothold; whether to allow the Devil to expand his control; whether to stop resisting and give the Devil free rein. In the end, there may be precious little moral freedom left to someone who is in Satan's grip; but even so, that person first had to make choices that opened the door for his influence. This is why in the Ananias and Sapphira incident, Peter can describe them as having a heart "filled" by Satan and yet also say, "How is it that *you* have contrived this deed in your heart?" (Acts 5:3–4, emphasis added). Ananias

> *In light of the superior power of God and the saving work of Christ, Satan need not ever have control of anyone's life.*

and Sapphira are *both* in Satan's grip *and* morally responsible for their own actions, which may make for a helpful parallel to our earlier discussion of how we can be both under divine direction and fully responsible for our own actions.

Does the first-century perspective on the demonic still make any sense twenty centuries later? Many people, especially those influenced by the science and rationalism of the Enlightenment, rejected any notion of the Devil as simply metaphorical or mythological, a kind of primitive human personification of evil that must now be left behind.

Many Christians, especially those most attracted to the kind of divine determinism discussed earlier, also shy away from acknowledging the considerable biblical treatment of a demonic realm. As early as Augustine, Christian thinkers have strongly resisted any kind of cosmic dualism in which the heavenly realm is populated by two fairly equal powers battling it out for control of human affairs. They want to find a way to subordinate the biblical picture of Satan within a perspective that emphasizes God's unquestionable and unchallengeable power. Other contemporary Christians are turned off by the naïveté and gullibility of a certain Christian fringe that sees the Devil around every corner, the kind of view promoted by certain dubious TV evangelists and other unappealing characters. This strikes many thoughtful people as a worldview for hayseeds and bumpkins, and they want no part of it.

All of that being said, there are still Jeffrey Dahmer and Adolf Hitler and Joseph Stalin and Idi Amin and Osama bin Ladin and many garden-variety molesters and swindlers and abusers and murderers and liars. It is not difficult to spot the domination of evil in their lives. Further, we don't have to look at the world's greatest practitioners of evil to become uncomfortably and very personally familiar with the process of temptation, the gradual or sudden collapse of moral resistance, and the growth of moral and spiritual illness or even evil in our hearts and lives. *Many of us have seen evil up close, and we do not make light of it.* Maybe some don't feel comfortable personifying this process or imagining a cosmic realm in which demons lick their chops at the thought of devouring us. After many years studying Adolf Hitler and Nazism, I myself have returned to a decisive reclaiming of the New Testament depiction of a personal Satan. It's not just that Hitler and some of his top aides flirted with the occult but more that any close study of his life finds his dark soul, and his dark powers over people, the most remarkable thing about him. And the ultimate effects were devastating beyond words. However this issue is resolved, few among us can deny that there is something very real and very true about the reality of demonic power, however it is understood. It does not destroy the reality of our freedom or the meaningfulness of our choices or the power and sovereignty of God; it does, though, show us what can happen when we open our hearts and lives to sin and finally to evil.[4]

ADDICTIONS AND COMPULSIONS

While fewer people are willing to embrace the concept of a literal Devil these days than in earlier times, it would be surprising if the description of how the Devil gains a foothold in our lives is entirely unfamiliar to those who have considered the phenomenon of addictive and compulsive behavior.

Whether the problem is trips to the convenience store to buy junk food or compulsive handwashing or addictive gambling or self-mutilation or pornography or alcoholism or rage or smoking or drug abuse, there is plenty of evidence that human nature is susceptible to habitual destructive behavior. These destructive habits find (or create) a chink in our armor, gain a foothold, and if unimpeded can take over more and more of our behavior. If this sounds uncomfortably familiar, consider the dictionary definitions of *addiction* and *compulsion*. An addiction is "the state of being given up or having yielded to a habit or practice to such an extent that ceasing the behavior causes severe discomfort." A compulsion, similarly, is "a strong and often irresistible impulse to perform an act contrary to one's own will." In either case, the addictive or compulsive person gradually loses the freedom to do anything else besides what he or she is doing. Impulses override will, or will is taken over or yields to habits that become so deeply entrenched that they are irreversible (or nearly so).

Addiction is one of the most pitiful of human experiences. We become accustomed to seeing ourselves or others in addictive patterns but would do well to step back and look at what a sorry state of affairs addiction really is. I think of the many people I have known who light up cigarette after cigarette, fully knowing the destructive impact of what they are doing but fully unable to stop doing it. The same thing is true with overeating, drinking, and dozens of other practices. Addiction leads to a progressive and sometimes complete loss of freedom. The habit controls the person, rather than the reverse—often with disastrous consequences. We lose our freedom and wholeness, since the habit takes over so much of body, mind, spirit, and soul.

Of course, scientists can now tell us about how addictions alter brain chemistry. But long before science could look into the brain, moral thinkers had developed an account of how moral freedom is lost and how addictions and compulsions gain control of a life. Aristotle said that "we are what we habitually do." Human beings tend to exercise their freedom in such a way that they establish patterns and structures of behavior that are rooted in habitual practices. Whatever we do regularly enough becomes habit-forming, whether reading the morning paper or drinking a cup of coffee or waking for morning prayer or beating our children or whatever else. Diet books tell us that if we do something for just forty days in a row, it will likely become entrenched as a habit in our lives—for good or for ill. That's why most diet plans or self-reinvention schemes involve practices that are designed to reshape our habits over a certain period of time. It is more than a bit striking that it takes just forty days to form a habit that can govern behavior for a lifetime.

We will look more deeply at habit formation in the next chapter, when we discuss how we can become morally good people. For now, we see once again that our freedom is not absolute but is instead constrained, in this case by the habits that we form. We act not so much in a series of free, separate individual choices but instead in structured patterns of behavior that reflect our habits and determine the direction we take on life's journey. Unless we are mentally ill, most of us are at first relatively free to develop the habits that come to structure our behavior. But once habits are in place, we are not entirely free to change them or to depart from what these habits lead us to do.

> *We act not so much in a series of free, separate individual choices but instead in structured patterns of behavior that reflect our habits and determine the direction we take on life's journey.*

FATE, DESTINY, CHANCE, LUCK

For centuries, people in many cultures have believed that a mysterious, transpersonal, and yet neither divine nor demonic force called variously *fate* or *destiny,* or perhaps *chance* or *luck,* determines the course of events.

In the Western world, at least, fate and luck have a discernible intellectual and cultural history. Before Christian belief came to dominate Western culture, many people ascribed to fate or destiny what deterministic Christians later ascribed to God. Fate in this sense is simply another word for God (or "the gods"), both representing that unknowable, all-powerful force that determines all events and predetermines our destinies. If a difference is apparent between pagan fatalism and Christian determinism, it may be that the pagan (pre-Christian) belief in fate lacked the element of hopefulness found in at least some versions of Christian determinism. Christians believed in a personal God with an interest in human beings and a somewhat benign nature, whereas fate was entirely impersonal and even "blind." The idea was basically that our lives take place under the domination of impersonal forces that could just as readily destroy us as cause us to prosper, and there is nothing anyone can do about it.

Once Christian beliefs began to weaken in the Western world, the concept of fate or destiny made a reappearance. It is certainly apparent in Shakespeare's plays, for example, in which fate is often depicted as determining the tragic course of events just before all the characters end up dead on the stage. Today, it is easy to see the resurgence of the concept of fate or destiny, especially in matters of the heart. People are far less likely to see God as directing the course of all events than they were some years ago, but they are also increasingly unwilling to accept any purely rationalistic or scientific explanation for why things happen as they do. All reason, all science, and no God makes for a universe too cold, too unfeeling, to endure. Nor are people quite as willing to accept personal moral responsibility for their own choices in life as they once were some years ago. For all those reasons, many people commonly ascribe to fate or destiny the responsibility for their romances, their marriages, their affairs, their divorces—in other words, for the outcome of their life journeys. This desire for a reenchanted, mystical, even supernatural but not Christian worldview also helps us make sense of the growing interest in astrology, another ancient (pre-Christian, precritical, premodern) practice that has become very popular in recent times. With astrology, our stars determine our fate, and yet knowing the requisite information gives us at least some control by enabling us to make astrologically informed choices. And so we read our horoscopes and plan our days!

All reason, all science, and no God makes for a universe too cold, too unfeeling, to endure.

Belief in chance or luck is a less hopeful yet still essentially deterministic approach to understanding how or why things happen as they do. If either God or fate determines what happens, at least somebody or something is in charge. But if luck or chance is at the helm, nobody or nothing is in charge. Chance is the absence of any predictable, discernable, changeable, controllable, or even understandable reason for what happens. Chance or luck is pure random accident, with life determined by freakish, arbitrary, happenstance events. In this view, humans are not free because all is randomness. In the end, belief in chance reflects a deeply pessimistic worldview, even if one happens to believe that one's luck is good most of the time. Thoughtful Christians can, I believe, acknowledge a certain degree of randomness in life's events. If I roll threes rather than sixes on the dice (playing Monopoly, not roulette, let us say!) or draw two aces rather than three of a kind in a friendly game of poker, this is luck and nothing but. Beyond this, however, Christians are generally uninterested in ascribing either human choices or any other significant aspects of life to the vagaries of chance, nor should they be. Yet those who do make such attributions downplay the significance of human freedom while elevating the power of other causes and forces.

HEREDITY AND GENES

As we discussed earlier in this book, there is no doubt that our genetic heritage and our upbringing are significant in determining who we become, how we handle our relationships with other people, the effectiveness of our moral compass, and just about every other aspect of our lives. In our families, we learn language, observe relationships, give and receive love (or do not), acquire tastes and preferences, listen to conversations, are inculcated with a worldview, are subtly directed toward particular vocational paths, learn what it means to be a man or a woman, are trained in various particular skills, and so on.

Given my own upbringing, it was very likely that I would enjoy books, baseball, and the beach and not care much for NASCAR, pork rinds, and hockey. It was very likely that I would go to college, marry, and have a white-collar job and unlikely that I would drop out of school, remain single, and work in a factory. My upbringing, like yours, made certain choices more probable and others quite improbable. We are not surprised when the children of sports stars end up making their way up the athletic ladder, but we would be surprised if, say, a tough NFL linebacker's son became an opera singer.

The ever-developing science of genetics offers the promise of another way of understanding and explaining the origins of human behavior. It is now widely believed that genes, and combinations or networks of genes, "code for" certain tendencies and conditions, especially various health conditions. It's not certain that genes that code for a wide range of human behaviors and traits will be found, but scientists are looking into the matter. Some members of the scientific community believe that someday most significant behavioral tendencies and patterns will be decoded and linked to particular genes in the human genome. But the most careful geneticists remain cautious in their claims about what genetic science will ever be able to tell us about what causes or helps determine most aspects of human behavior.

Even so, however, when one considers the deep impact of upbringing and the possible impact of genetic predispositions—not to mention the dynamic combination of both genetics and upbringing—it is clear that these aspects of who we are affect our freedom to make significant moral choices. Certainly it is not surprising that some people have embraced the belief that freedom is illusory and that we are what we come from.

Yet we also don't have to go very far to find counter-evidence for this view. We all know children raised in the same household by the same parents who turn out very differently from one another. Most of us are aware even of identical twins whose lives take very different courses, not to mention other genetically related people whose lives bear no resemblance at all. The way in which upbringing, and perhaps genetic predisposition, shapes and constrains the range of choices we make is impressive. It would be foolhardy in light of available evidence to suppose that any of us are absolutely free to make our choices apart from such influences. But still we all have seen the way that human choices do vary. They simply cannot be reduced to the sum of genetic and familial factors. We are indeed free—not as free as some people have supposed us to be, but also not the genetically driven or childhood-driven automatons that some people suggest. Our choices are constrained within a certain range, but within that range they remain ours to make.

SIN—AGAIN

Perhaps the most powerful challenge within Christian tradition to the concept of real human moral freedom is the belief that our sinful nature determines our choices. Our fallen condition means that we will sin: we are not free not to sin. But if we are not free not to sin, then how can it meaningfully be said that we are free at all? Here the issues we discussed in Chapter Four on sin and human nature resurface.

This line of thinking has a long and tortuous history in Christian thought. For our purposes here, it's most useful to contrast two of the primary competing perspectives, the Calvinist and the Catholic.

The Calvinist stance (again, from John Calvin, whose ideas on determinism we discussed earlier in the chapter) asserts that were it not for salvation through Jesus Christ and its transforming power, human beings would invariably choose evil. Despite evidences of God's will available in creation, despite a nagging internal sense of right and wrong, itself implanted in all people by God, the "unregenerate" or unsaved person will ignore or distort these evidences and choose the wrong. Making reference to the Christian theologians Origen and Augustine, Calvin put it this way: "Origen seems to have put forward a definition [of free will] generally agreed upon among ecclesiastical writers when he said that it is a faculty of the reason to distinguish between good and evil [and] a faculty of the will to choose one or the other. Augustine does not disagree with this when he teaches that it is a faculty of the reason and the will to choose good with the assistance of grace; evil, when grace is absent."[5] The biblical scholar Byron Curtis clarifies this assertion in the following way: "[The] Reformed definition of free will: 'The power to choose according to one's strongest motive, nature, and character.' In the unregenerate, to freely choose evil. In the regenerate, to freely choose God and the good."[6]

This stance clearly has the implication that only "regenerate" people—that is, only people who have been "born again" in a saving experience with Jesus Christ—have the capacity to choose the good. Everyone else is bound to sin, not free to do otherwise. It is as if, wherever they think they are going on life's journey, their destination is sin and the eternal judgment it will bring. To the objection that people can hardly be held morally responsible for what they cannot avoid doing, Calvinists would say that human beings are guilty for the sinful condition that is itself the cause of this unvarying propensity to choose evil and for the many wrong choices that flow from that condition. The fact that God chooses to save some (but not all) from eternal perdition is grace enough to contemplate over a hundred lifetimes.

Still, this is a staggeringly pessimistic vision of the human condition apart from Christ. No one who has not been saved can choose the good. All are trapped, enslaved, bound to sin. The only free person is the Christian, and this freedom is contingent on the Holy Spirit's directing the regenerated sinner to God and the good. Everyone else is essentially a sin addict who cannot choose or find wholeness and whose life will end in eternal (and often earthly) destruction.

The Catholic stance is not quite so dark. Catholic thought is by no means utopian or optimistic about the human condition. We are indeed all sinners, and our sinfulness has morally devastating consequences. However, the Catholic tradition tends toward a greater optimism about the surviving remnant of our moral capacity despite the impact of sin. Reason and will—the capacity to *think* rightly and to *choose* rightly—remain central, but the Catholic stance is that these capacities have not been entirely corrupted by sin. "It is not easy for man, wounded by sin, to maintain moral balance," the church acknowledges. However, human virtues can be "acquired by education, by deliberate acts, and by a perseverance ever-renewed in repeated efforts."[7] It is not easy to make right choices, though the formation of good habits helps, as do religious and moral education and a sustained effort to do the right thing. Besides such efforts, living rightly is greatly aided by the "purifying" and "elevating" effects of divine grace. Catholics want to maintain that even nonbelievers are aided by divine grace when their reason and will function properly (as they sometimes do, as when unbelieving parents treat their children with tenderness and love). This grace is operating even if the unbeliever refuses to acknowledge it. But the bottom line here is that it is possible to make right choices, apart from explicit commitment to Jesus Christ and involvement in the community of faith, because every human being has the surviving moral capacity, however fragile and fallible, to do the right thing.

This helps make sense of the very existence of moral codes, and legal systems based on moral codes, in every civilization in human history. Obviously, members of other civilizations were not and are not all regenerate Christians, but most have somehow known that murder, rape, and stealing are wrong. This concept also makes sense of those non-Christians we know, even those who claim allegiance to no faith at all, who live according to a serious and upright moral code themselves. Perhaps such people are exceptional, but they do exist, even as there is plenty of evidence of supposed Christians whose behavior shows little evidence of the "elevating and purifying" effects of God's grace.

The Catholic stance is that this is a both-and rather than an either-or situation. Both the surviving elements of our God-given moral capacity and the grace of God in Christ together make up the ingredients of a person capable of the highest and most refined moral choices. It is not for the church to tell unbelievers that they have no moral capacity for good whatsoever but rather to tell them that they will find the fulfillment of that capacity only in Christ and that only in him can people find eternal salvation and forgiveness of the sins they do commit.

In this way, we once again find it possible to defend the existence of human moral freedom, even among those who do not know Christ. In the orthodox tradition of the Christian faith, we affirm as we did in Chapter Four that we are all sinners embedded in sinful social structures, that over the course of a lifetime we will certainly sin, that no person is entirely free of sin other than Jesus, that we are susceptible to developing sinful patterns of behavior, and that we all need the redeeming grace of God in Jesus Christ. And yet by God's grace we do have a surviving capacity either to choose the right or the wrong. Christians enjoy the rich assurance that with the help of God's Spirit, we can be trained to choose the right ever more frequently, but this does not require the belief that those apart from an explicit relationship with Christ will choose the wrong every time. Freedom, once again, survives, as a capacity of all human beings. With the early church father John Chrysostom, we affirm, "God, having placed good and evil in our power, has given us full freedom of choice"—as long as we understand that to mean a freedom constrained, but not destroyed, by the effects of sin.[8]

THE PRECIOUS, FRAGILE GIFT OF MORAL FREEDOM

Every human community offers moral instruction. Parents teach their children. Schoolteachers exhort their pupils. Priests and pastors lead their congregations. Police officers chide law-breakers. Politicians paint word pictures of what a morally good community would look like.

The vocabulary of "should" has never been, and can never be, erased from the human experience. We "should" do X and "should not" do Y, and the most strenuous efforts are made to train us in doing X and avoiding Y. It is hard to imagine any human society without such efforts.

Those who deny the existence of the human freedom to make real moral choices would have to consider this entire moral teaching enterprise to be a waste of time, wouldn't they? Moral exhortation is senseless if moral freedom does not exist. Moral accountability is senseless if people are not free to make moral choices for which they can be held accountable. The implication would be that parents, teachers, pastors, priests, and everyone else who provides such moral instruction should just close up shop and let God, Satan, addiction, fate, chance, genes, upbringing, or our sinful nature determine what we do. But we cannot accept this denial of real human freedom, either on biblical grounds or based on a broad observation of the human condition.

That is not to say that there are not a number of factors that limit, constrain, and shape our freedom. From a Christian perspective, it cannot be said that we are absolutely free to make our choices or determine the course of our lives

- Because God is sovereign, powerful, and involved in directing human life
- Because Satan is real, seeking and sometimes gaining control over our choices if we give him a foothold
- Because our choices harden into habits that structure our actions, sometimes into destructive addictions and compulsions
- Because there is at least a small element of chance in human affairs
- Because we are deeply affected by our genetic predispositions and other physical factors, as well as by our childhood upbringing and other relational influences
- Because our sinful nature inclines us to reason and choose wrongly

If we look at this list, we must conclude that human moral freedom is a precious, fragile gift. In Christian terms, our moral freedom is a gift that comes from God and is apparent in human life from the very origins of the species. Surely this is an implication of the story of Adam and Eve, who misused their freedom—but that means they had freedom available to misuse.

Having moral freedom means that although we do not create ourselves *ex nihilo* (out of nothing), we do have some capacity to participate in molding the wet clay of a self that is given to us by God, nature, parents, and history. This clay does not remain altogether wet and moldable for long; as we make our choices, we develop habits and the self begins to take on a definite shape. There is always the possibility of a shattering destruction of the existing self and reshaping of a new self—this is, in part, the meaning of religious conversion, and it can occur for the worse rather than the better. But for most of us, our selves harden (for good or ill) into a certain recognizable shape by the time we reach adulthood, formed by a combination of what others gave to us and what we have done with what they gave to us.

Human freedom, we can now see, is a fragile gift because it can so easily be lost—to Satan's wiles, to addictions, to sinful habits, or even to an upbringing so vicious and destructive that it swamps a wounded child's best efforts to lead a constructive life as an adult. But even in the best case it is clear that whatever freedom we have is not entirely ours to do with as we please, for if we make bad choices and misuse our freedom, we become enslaved to behaviors that harm ourselves and others. Freedom is not freedom if it spirals downward into license, vice, addiction, evil, and self-destruction.

The very nature of these conditions and restraints leads to the conclusion that human beings are sufficiently vulnerable to a misuse of the freedom we have that we must look not for the total freedom of personal autonomy but for the right guide to direct us in our life journeys.[9] It is as if, assessing our situation and considering our vulnerability to wrong choices and destructive patterns, we decide to take the gift of freedom that is ours and somehow offer it back to the Giver.

Show me, we say, what to do with this freedom so that it is a force for good rather than evil in my life. We end up with the paradoxical affirmation of the Christian tradition that the freest person is the one who has given his or her freedom back to God. It is this God who knows what the freest, most satisfying, and most virtuous human life is supposed to look like—because he designed us in the first place. Philip Turner's words make a nice summary of our sojourn in this chapter—and of life's journey: "It is . . . God's gift of freedom that makes possible the great drama of our lives, a drama in which God himself takes hold of us, wrestles with our stubborn will, and teaches us in our very freedom to love rightly and steadfastly."[10]

6

How Do I Become a Good Person?

It is in Christ, Redeemer and Savior, that the divine image, disfigured in man by the first sin, has been restored to its original beauty and ennobled by the grace of God.

—*Catechism of the Catholic Church*

In the summer of 2004, I read the surprising news that the notorious prizefighter Mike Tyson is trying to make a fresh start with his life. The man voted by *Sports Illustrated* readers as the worst role model in the history of sports would like to change both his image and the reality behind it. In representative comments from one interview, he said, "I've been working on forgiveness. Life is too short to hold grudges. There's not enough time. Every second I'm closer to my death. I'm trying to do the things to make me the most successful and to manage my life properly, which is something I've never done."[1]

When even Mike Tyson, the man who bit off a piece of Evander Holyfield's ear during their 1997 prize fight, wants to become a good person, you know that something significant is going on. It is striking that during the same news cycle, the

Artist Formerly Known as Prince—now once again known as Prince and a recent convert to the Jehovah's Witnesses—announced that he was cleaning up his act and would be singing "only songs that I wouldn't be embarrassed for my children to hear."

Just what is going on here?

We are catching a glimpse of another fundamental dimension of human nature that we have been exploring in this book: the perennial human quest to get this life right—to become a better person and to find wholeness through rich internal moral growth. Despite the many dark and foreboding descriptions of human nature in the Bible, some of which we have already discussed, it turns out that sinful humans are often interested in getting better, being different, turning their lives around, finding the right path. Perhaps they come to view this reclamation as the change necessary to reach other goals in their life journeys, such as successful relationships, happiness, or even eternal life with God. They want to clean themselves up in order to change the essence of their lives. Or perhaps they embrace moral reclamation as the destination itself—in other words, personal moral transformation becomes the goal of the journey, not just the means. For whatever reason, many of us seek to become better people at a certain point in our lives. It's worth asking why and what that impulse means—and that is what we'll be doing in this chapter.

THE PRODIGAL SON

This instinct for redemption, for turning our lives around, has made the story of the Prodigal Son (Luke 15:11–32) much loved for two thousand years. This amazing story of a young rebel who abandons his father only to find his way back home again is an extended parable with meanings that can be found at multiple levels. In its literary context, it is clearly a story about the character of God, the One who forgives straying rebels and welcomes them back home. It is also a story of hardhearted (self-)righteous "older brother" types who so often resist the demonstrations of grace that are offered to prodigals and rebels.

But it is also an all too common story about life's journey. The younger son who walks away from a good and prosperous life with his family, wastes his inheritance on wild partying, and then finally "comes to himself" and staggers back home sounds familiar. Many of us have stories to tell of our own prodigal years, our days of folly, in which we turned our backs on faith, family, and morality and went wild—some more than others. Perhaps it is your story.

Yet something in us leads us back home. Most of us are saddened by the sight of the aging rock star, with ex-wife (or ex-wives) and children, still doing drugs and getting smashed, unable or unwilling to pull himself together and be a grown-up. We know that after a while, there can be little excuse for choosing the prodigal's path. As it says in the book of Proverbs, "Wisdom cries out in the street; in the squares she raises her voice. At the busiest corner she cries out" (2:20); and when she does, she cries out our names, and it's hard not to hear her, although some of us stubbornly block her out. As we survey the wreckage created by our bad choices, after a while only a fool can continue to resist the obvious truth.

But recognition that we have made bad choices and need a new direction is the beginning and not the end of the process. Perhaps in our culture, so steeped in the sentiments of an old standard like the hymn "Amazing Grace," we seem to know what to make of the moment of repentance and the desire for a fresh start. But we don't know so well what to do once we get past that point. We know how to say, as the tax collector in Luke 18 said, "God have mercy on me, a sinner," but not really how to change so that we can stop having to pray that prayer all the time. This chapter is a reflection on what it might look like to grow into a morally solid person, a morally good person— not perfect, not sinless, certainly not a snob, not self-righteous, not a smug elder-brother type but a genuinely good and admirable and whole human being, a person of integrity and maturity.

> *We know how to say, "God have mercy on me, a sinner," but not really how to change so that we can stop having to pray that prayer all the time.*

In the Christian tradition, there are four basic approaches to the question of how one becomes a good person. One emphasizes God's forgiveness of people who don't really change very much, a second focuses on change through hard moral effort, a third stresses the power of religious conversion to transform lives, and the last envisions a process of gradual moral formation. I think the first three contain truths but are flawed, because they each misunderstand something important about human nature. But taken together and synthesized correctly, they give us a vision of moral goodness arrived at through gradual moral formation into the image of Jesus Christ, who makes possible the restoration in us of the image of God in all of its fullness.

"CHRISTIANS AREN'T PERFECT, JUST FORGIVEN"

The sentiment of being not perfect but forgiven is not as common on bumper stickers as it once was, but it's still a popular slogan among many Christians. It can still be found on T-shirts and mugs in your local Christian bookstore. And it remains both profoundly right and profoundly wrong.

Taken at face value, there is nothing untruthful about the statement that "Christians aren't perfect, just forgiven." Both clauses are true. Christians are *not* perfect, because they remain sinners. And they *are* forgiven, because Jesus has paid the price for their sins. If they have responded in faith and commitment, they are Christians, forgiven and yet imperfect.

But there is a kind of saucy nonchalance about moral imperfection in this slogan that is profoundly wrongheaded. (I might feel this way because I've been cut off by too many rude and imperfect Christian drivers sporting this bumper sticker—but I forgive them!)

Those who take the Bible seriously should understand that sin is not a small concern. As we have seen, it wrecks lives, disrupts God's creation, ruins relationships, and cost God a great price to redeem. Christians should be the first in line to acknowledge that our own "imperfection," and the wrongs that pervade the whole world, are serious business. We ought not to rest easy with the reality of ongoing sin in our lives. For many generations and in many places, Christians worked strenuously to uproot sinful actions and thoughts from their lives. But this spirit is almost completely absent among us today. Instead we nonchalantly claim God's forgiveness—as if forgetting the bloody sacrifice that made it possible—and go on with our morally mediocre lives. No wonder Dietrich Bonhoeffer accused the church of peddling "cheap grace."[2]

There is a strand of Christian thought that is much more serious about sin than this, but in the end it reaches the same conclusion. These folks could sport the same bumper sticker not because they take sin lightly but precisely because they take it so seriously. These are the Christians from traditions that believe that the Bible teaches that we can expect to make little or no progress against sin in our lives as long as we are here in these bodies and on this earth.

Martin Luther, the leader of the Protestant Reformation in the sixteenth century, is often quoted to this effect, to some extent unfairly.[3] He was certainly very deeply impressed by the wretchedness of sin—no nonchalance there. But he believed that what God has done with sin through Jesus Christ is to forgive it. He did offer strenuous exhortations to Christians to obey Jesus and live righteously. But he sadly confessed that not one in a thousand so-called Christians is a true one, in the sense of fully obeying the teachings of Jesus. The heart of the Christian message is not that somehow Jesus changes human nature but that Jesus makes forgiveness available to us, wretched sinners that we all are. We remain sinners, but, by God's grace, by faith, through the blood of Christ, we can be forgiven.

> *The heart of the Christian message is not that somehow Jesus changes human nature but that Jesus makes forgiveness available to us, wretched sinners that we all are.*

Still, there was more to it for Luther. Having come through the Catholic monastic tradition, with its great seriousness about sin and its careful cataloguing of particular sins (and their various punishments), Luther was convinced that this whole approach put the believer's attention on himself rather than on Christ. Luther argued, as the Christian thinkers Bruce Birch and Larry Rasmussen put it, that the goal of the Christian life should be to move not from vice to virtue "but from both vice *and* virtue to grace."[4] Emphasizing human efforts to overcome sin and attain virtue, Luther feared, leads to self-centeredness, pride, and dependence on self rather than dependence on God. We can spend all our time in morbid (or self-congratulatory) introspection rather than gratitude to God and service to our neighbors. So while we think about how we are doing with lust or greed, our neighbor's house burns down and we don't notice.

That is why to this day the tenor of a classic Lutheran worship service remains as it was in Luther's day. The goal of the worship leader is to "preach the Gospel," which means to tell people that they are sinners who deserve eternal separation from God but for whom Christ has died. Those who believe are saved by God's grace alone through their faith. The goal is to produce people who embrace this grace-gift and live their lives with an astonished sense of themselves as forgiven sinners—not morally good people but bad people whom God loves anyway. The key virtue relevant to such a person is gratitude for an unmerited gift. It is this gratitude, and the faith that lies at its foundation, that is then encouraged week by week in the church's life and worship.

Luther certainly understood the miracle and wonder of God's forgiving grace. Yet as the twentieth-century American theologian Reinhold Niebuhr—himself a thinker nurtured within the Lutheran tradition—put it many decades ago, this

stance can easily reduce the whole of God's grace to pardon
or forgiveness. The New Testament itself reveals that God's
grace is experienced both as *forgiveness* and as *power*—the
power to change. God does not just pardon; he liberates. He
does not just acquit; he transforms.[5] Both are themes in the
New Testament, and the abandonment of the theme of transformation has had disastrous effects both in the church and
in a culture deeply affected by the church's own shallow
understanding of the power to change made available in Jesus
Christ.[6] It has led to a deep moral mediocrity, as Christians
have failed to make significant moral progress, their lives
indistinguishable from their non-Christian neighbors in a
morally confused culture.

"I THINK I CAN, I THINK I CAN"

At the other end of the spectrum from a pure grace and forgiveness model is what might be called the "I think I can, I
think I can" approach—like the "Little Engine That Could"
in the popular children's story. In this kind of approach to
a changed life, the emphasis is on sheer willpower and raw
determination, on working harder and becoming more moral
through our own efforts. Think New Year's resolutions, and
you'll know what I am talking about.

The self-help section of any bookstore these days offers
numerous "I think I can" books. Whether the issue is diet,
self-esteem, divorce recovery, or parenting, a variety of five-
and seven- and ten- and twelve-step programs are on offer.
They promise readers that if they will just give these programs their very best efforts, success is sure to follow. (My
current "I think I can" book is called *Banish Your Belly,* which
perhaps tells you more than you want to know about me.)

There is certainly some truth to the claims of these self-help books. The goal of achieving real change in our lives, and the belief that such change is genuinely possible, is an advance over the imperfect-but-forgiven stance we have just considered. It is also definitely true that hard work is a part of any process of personal growth. Willpower—the energetic determination to do the right things and make the right choices—is indeed important to success in life. Willpower can help us overcome inertia, resistance, and sin and move us toward accomplishing our goals.

But most of us who have attempted to achieve some kind of objective purely on the basis of teeth-gritting effort have soon discovered the frustrating limits of our willpower. We know what we ought to do, even what we want to do, but the inner forces of resistance are just too strong. We are impotent in the face of our own bad habits, our laziness, and our comfort with our current way of living. We are aware that we need an infusion of power in order to defeat these forces and achieve our goals. Otherwise our New Year's resolutions are abandoned a few days into January.

The Christian tradition, rooted in the Bible's teachings, has been consistent in claiming that the human will is unable to accomplish its own good apart from the help of God. "I can do all things," Paul says, "through Christ who strengthens me" (Philippians 4:13). The triune God—Father, Son, and Holy Spirit—is depicted as the ultimate source of power for any good that Christians accomplish and any growth that we achieve. Paul is especially realistic about how difficult it is to grow and get it right even with the power of the Holy Spirit at work in our lives. That's what he is agonizing about in Romans 7: "The good that I would do, I do not; the evil that I would not do, that I do." If this is the case even for Paul, how much more unrealistic is it to think that the rest of us will be able to become morally good and mature people apart from the active intervention of God in our lives? No, we are going to need some kind of external power source to move our vehicle toward moral growth in life's journey.

"I ONCE WAS BLIND
BUT NOW I SEE"

As early as the eighteenth century, preachers traveled throughout the colonized portions of the North American continent, proclaiming the need for authentic conversion to faith in Jesus Christ. Quite often, a major part of their message was that such a conversion would also bring about dramatic changes in the convert's emotional, moral, and family life. In other words, conversion meant not just changed beliefs but changed lives. The power of God that was demonstrated in personal salvation was also available for personal transformation.

There can be no question that personal religious conversion leading to dramatic moral change is a significant motif in our religious history.

At its best, this movement (known as revivalism because of its emphasis on reviving Christian faith) was a major force for both personal and social change in early American life. Thousands and thousands of people believed the preachers' message that Jesus meant to transform his followers' lives. Some revivalists, such as Charles Finney, had rich and wide-ranging moral messages (especially, though not exclusively, for men), imploring listeners to come to Christ and having done

so to abandon slavery, treat women with respect, stop drinking, be kind to the poor, start caring for their children, and
generally change their lives for the better. There can be no
question that personal religious conversion leading to dramatic moral change is a significant motif in our religious history. "I once was blind but now I see"—famous words from
our most beloved hymn, "Amazing Grace"—aptly symbolizes
the moral transformation revivalists proclaimed and expected.

This tradition of moral transformation through conversion also has clear biblical roots. A deep vein of the biblical
record is confrontation of sin and sinner by the powerful
proclamation of divine truth, leading to dramatic religious
awakening and a changed life. In the book of Samuel in the
Old Testament, the prophet Nathan confronted King David
after David's horrendous chain of sins: adultery with Bath-
sheba; the arranged murder of her husband, Uriah; and the
cover-up of both. When Nathan finds a way to reach David's
heart and challenge him for his sins, David is struck to the
depths of his soul. He knows that he has done wrong and is
willing to pay the price for his sins. Here David does not experience religious conversion, as if only now is he coming to
believe in God, but he does experience a profound sorrow
for his sins that leads to repentance and change in the way he
lives his life.

In the book of Luke in the New Testament, John the
Baptist proclaims his fiery message of repentance for sin, and
people repent in droves. He tells them specifically what they
are to do to change, and they commit to doing it. Jesus has
the same effect on many others: he calls tax collectors and
prostitutes to him, and they abandon their former sins as they
follow him. Perhaps the most famous convert of all is Paul
himself, who goes from being a murderous persecutor of
Christians to being the leading apostle in the early church.

Perhaps Paul's dramatic experience of conversion on the road to Damascus has most deeply shaped the revivalist tradition. If it could happen to him, it can happen to anyone. Paul himself certainly believed that, and revival preachers have been saying the same thing for centuries, to this day.

The reality of religious conversion and the subsequent experience of moral transformation, then, fit with a strand of the Bible; they are beloved aspects of our religious heritage, and they continue to make a great difference in many lives today. They provide the encouraging hope that no one is too far gone, no one is beyond redemption, and the power of God can reach in and transform the life of anyone who is open to it.

But those of us who have spent our lives within revivalist traditions also know the very real limits of this approach, at least as it is often handled in our churches.

First, the "I once was blind but now I see" paradigm doesn't really apply to children, teenagers, and others who have been raised in and faithfully live the Christian tradition. What do you tell someone who has never been "blind" in any obvious way, never been the prodigal away on a sinful binge in a far country, but instead is a pretty responsible twelve-year-old who just wants to understand more fully the faith he has embraced from childhood? What if this child cannot recall a specific dramatic moment when he crossed over from darkness to light, sin to repentance, and unbelief to faith?

What tends to happen in such cases is that children and teenagers whose faith and moral character have been growing incrementally through the careful instruction of their parents and churches feel that they must manufacture some kind of dramatic conversion experience in order to be truly "saved." More than a few such young people have launched into a time of rebellion as if they needed it as validation for their later "conversion" and "transformation." Churchgoing young people who don't "get lost" also often experience an agonizing and pitiful quest for certainty about their salvation. Because they are unable to point to any dramatic conversion experience, they wonder whether they are really saved at all. In some extreme cases, this worry becomes a truly frightening and paralyzing obsession. The fact of the matter is that not everyone moves toward God or moral goodness through a darkness-to-light conversion experience. To establish that progression as the sole paradigm for religious experience can be devastating in many ways. While the New Testament says that faith alone saves and that all have sinned and are therefore in need of the salvation to which faith gains us access (see Matthew 3:2; Luke 3:13; Acts 2:37–38; Romans 3:21-26), the ways in which young people repent of sin, express faith, and come to commitment to Christ are often very different from the journeys taken by those who convert later in life.

Another major problem associated with the conversion and transformation approach is that it can lead to dramatic but shallow and ultimately fruitless conversions—or purported conversions. Everyone who is a part of a revivalist tradition is familiar with the pattern: if it's April, it must be revival time, and so you can count on old Joe to come walking down the aisle and saying he's found Jesus and is going to live right from now on. This feels good to the traveling evangelist, but everyone in the community knows that old Joe does this every year during revival week, and in the end he never changes at all—at least not for long. A dramatic "conversion" every now and then may become a substitute for the long, slow work of thoroughgoing personal transformation and moral growth that is supposed to flow from an authentic conversion experience. Conversion is at best a start on the moral journey. Even if it is a rocket-propelled start, the convert will need other resources to sustain the spiritual and moral journey toward wholeness over the long term.

So if these three approaches to the question of how we become "good people" are not quite adequate, where does that leave us? It is not good enough to say that "Christians aren't perfect, just forgiven," because it expects little or no moral growth. It is not good enough to say "I think I can," because willpower alone is unable to bring lasting moral growth. And it is not good enough to say "I once was blind but now I see," because dramatic personal turnarounds are not always how people grow morally, and they are surprisingly difficult to sustain. Is there a model for moral growth that can absorb the truths in each of these views while avoiding their weaknesses?

SLOWLY BUT SURELY

In my view, the most complete and workable model for how one grows into moral goodness emphasizes gradual moral growth in Jesus Christ. This incremental or developmental vision is very nicely expressed in the Roman Catholic tradition, especially as summarized in the catechism, which is used to teach Christian principles. This focus on the Catholic approach may seem surprising, coming from a Protestant author, but I think the day is long past when we can afford to ignore the best insights that emerge from sister Christian traditions. After study of a wide variety of alternatives, I am convinced that the Catholic account of the Christian moral life is the one that is most effective in avoiding the errors of the other approaches we have been discussing. It does not claim that moral growth is impossible. It does not reduce moral growth to willpower. And it does not place all of its eggs in the basket of religious conversion.

Instead, it offers a vision of life in Christ that is rooted in the creation of human beings in God's image and that calls us to joyful relationship with our Creator. It fully acknowledges the role of the human person's choice not just to believe in Jesus Christ but to direct our lives to the wholeness that is possible only in relationship to him and his will. "Human beings make their own contribution to their interior growth," by their "deliberate actions," the church says, and yet it is "with the help of grace [that] they grow into virtue" and "avoid sin." If they sin, they are not casual about it but they also do not panic, because, "like the prodigal son," they "entrust themselves to the mercy of our Father in heaven." In gratitude for God's forgiving love, they "attain to the perfection of charity." In other words, their growing virtue does not become a noxious self-righteousness because it is leavened by a humble gratitude for the love of God, which is then offered to other humble sinners as well. To understand how helpful this vision of moral goodness is, let's take its various elements one by one.[7]

MADE IN THE IMAGE OF GOD, CALLED TO RELATIONSHIP WITH GOD

The starting point for the Catholic vision of moral growth is the concept of humans made in the image of God, a concept with which we have been working since the beginning of this book. It plays itself out in some specific and highly relevant ways:

• The divine image in which we are made is present in every person and in every human relationship and experience of community. Deep within us is the dim awareness that we have a divine Creator and, somehow, a divinely ordained purpose and destiny for our journey in life. We were made for relationship with God and made to find our highest fulfillment in doing God's will. The Catholic church calls this our vocation to beatitude, or *blessedness.*

• Part of being made in God's image is that we "participate in the light and power of the divine Spirit." We have the rational capacity to understand "the order of things established by the Creator." We have the free will that makes us capable of directing ourselves toward the true good for which we were made. We also have the genuine freedom of mind and will to make morally meaningful choices.

• All human beings have the capacity to "recognize the voice of God," which urges us "to do what is good and avoid what is evil." This voice is heard in our conscience, which remains an operative power in human life and also reflects the divine image.

• Sin is real and has real consequences. It does not *destroy* our freedom or our moral capacity or the divine image in us as a whole, but it does damage it, and it does mean that we are "now inclined to evil and subject to error." There is a deep internal division in us. We may still desire what is good, but a contrary force within us pulls us in the other direction.

• The grace of God in Jesus Christ "delivered us from Satan and from sin." Therefore, "his grace restores what sin has damaged in us." Those who believe in Christ become sons and daughters of God. This transforms us by giving us the ability to follow Christ's example. We are capable of acting rightly, doing good, and maturing into holiness. The end of this path of spiritual and moral growth is "the glory of heaven," which is the ultimate destination of life's journey when rightly lived.

This set of assertions directly relates to the issues we have been wrestling with in other chapters, as well as our concerns in this one. It strongly emphasizes the surviving moral capacity of human beings, despite sin. This capacity includes our reason, our intellect, our will, our freedom, and our inborn desire to relate to the God who made us. Sin wounds our nature and inclines our will to evil and our thinking to error. The unredeemed sinner, however, is understood as a divided self rather than a self *wholly* inclined to evil. What Jesus Christ makes available, then, is deliverance from this condition of internal division, restoration of what sin has damaged, and therefore a return of all that God intended for us all along. As we grow in grace, our divided self becomes more and more whole, more and more "capable of acting rightly and doing good." Such growth in grace is only possible as we remain "in union with [our] Savior," as the catechism says. As we draw spiritually upon the power of Jesus Christ, with whom we are in deep and abiding relationship, new life blossoms in us. We grow in holiness and become more and more fitted for life in the eternal presence of God.

HUMAN FREEDOM AND RESPONSIBILITY

As the catechism says, "Freedom is the power, rooted in reason and will, to act or not to act, to do this or that, and so to perform deliberate actions on one's own responsibility."

Human beings are in this sense free, which is an aspect of being made in the divine image. Such freedom is part of our human dignity and rational capacity. God willed that human beings would be free, in part, so that they would freely choose to join their lives with his own. God could coerce our wills but chooses not to do so. Our freedom is one of the most exalted aspects of our nature and is "a force for growth and maturity in truth and goodness," as long as we exercise it rightly.

Human beings who have not yet "bound" their wills entirely over to God (or, presumably, to Satan or evil) remain free to choose between good and evil, right and wrong. We are fully responsible for the choices we make—at least the choices that are truly voluntary ones—and can be held accountable for them. Even unredeemed persons retain a level of freedom and the moral accountability that goes with it. The inclination to do wrong is real, but so also is the surviving reason, conscience, and moral sensitivity built into each human being because we are all made in God's image.

As we noted in Chapter Five, our freedom is fragile. If we repeatedly choose the wrong, we abuse our freedom. The end result is an erosion and finally a loss of our freedom and a descent into slavery to sin in its various forms: our will becomes bound, rather than free, with a seemingly irresistible inclination to choose the wrong continually. Perhaps this is the best way to describe Satan or an irredeemably evil person: he acts out a seemingly irresistible inclination to choose wrong. On the other hand, "the more one does what is good, the freer one becomes." Because "there is no true freedom except in the service of what is good and just," the repeated decision to choose the good sets us more and more free. Our ultimate desire should be to bind our will to God and the good he has established. In this way, we will be truly free—free from the desire to choose what is wrong and free from the negative effects of doing so. This is our quest, but it remains a struggle throughout life's journey.

A striking feature of the Catholic vision is its assertion, noted briefly in Chapter Five, that even those who do not acknowledge Jesus Christ retain some capacity to exercise their freedom rightly. They too can gain "progress in virtue" and "knowledge of the good" and can gain "mastery of the will" over their acts. However, this possibility of moral growth is greatly aided by Jesus Christ, and certainly that is God's plan for human wholeness. By his death on the cross he redeems us from sin and breaks its power over our will. He restores our freedom and enables us to experience a kind of liberty that has not been seen since before sin invaded God's good world.

> *Saved from our alienation from God and set free from bondage to sin, we are free to ascend—toward right choices, toward God, toward eternity.*

With restored freedom, believers are empowered to "make us free collaborators" in God's work in the world and in the church. Paul wrote that "for freedom Christ has set us free" (Galatians 5:1). The redeeming work of Christ has restored the original, glorious freedom that God intended human beings to have. Saved from our alienation from God and set free from bondage to sin, we are free to ascend—toward right choices, toward God, toward eternity. God joyfully welcomes us home as we choose him again and again, so often that it hardly seems like a choice at all.

RETRAINING THE MORAL SELF

Made for God and in God's image, we humans, whether Christian or not, are capable of choosing the good and the right, despite the damages of sin and the contradictory forces and internal resistance to doing and being what God made us to do and be. The affirmation of this surviving moral capacity enables us to understand how truly good people can be found all around the world, of many faiths and no faith, and also how it is that very diverse peoples and nations have been able to arrive at moral codes, judgments of right and wrong, and legal systems. And yet we affirm with Scripture that this real yet fragile moral capacity is greatly enhanced, even revolutionized, by encounter with the power of God in Jesus Christ. (We also affirm that the New Testament in Paul's letter to the Romans teaches that eternal salvation comes by grace through faith in Jesus Christ, apart from a good life and all of its works.) The Christian moral life, if reduced to a formula, could be described as follows:

Made in the image of God, with (damaged) God-given
    moral capacities
+ Moral resources available in Christ
+ Right exercise of moral freedom
= Sanctification, or gradual formation and eventually
    even transformation in Christ

But what are the particular elements of our God-given moral capacity that we can call on? How can our conscience, our passions, and our character traits contribute to our moral capacity? Each is part of our God-given standard equipment. Each has been damaged by sin. Their use and development are subject to the exercise of our freedom, which can be employed wisely or poorly. The best possible use of our freedom is to develop moral habits—reinforced by spiritual disciplines—that incline our will in the direction of choosing what is right and good.

The nature and function of *conscience* is as "a law inscribed in [our] heart by God," accessible through our reason, functioning as a kind of inner voice that approves choices that are good and denounces those that are evil. In the nineteenth century, Cardinal John Henry Newman described conscience as a messenger of God, a kind of internal rendering of God's voice. The concept of conscience received a remorseless pounding in the twentieth century as representatives of a variety of moral theories and worldviews fell all over each other to denounce its legitimacy. It was, variously, the voice of the bourgeois rich, externalized parental authority, the frustrated will to power, and much else, anything but what the Christian tradition said it was. But after the carnage of the last century, we should not be too sanguine about rejecting the concept of conscience. I believe it is both biblical and indispensable to the well-being of individuals and the human community.

Conscience, which Christians believe is both a part of every human spirit and also affected by the choices that people make, functions in a variety of ways. It gives us at least a dim perception of the principles of morality, as well as how these ought to be applied in particular circumstances. It provides evaluation or judgment of particular acts we have performed or are about to perform. It convicts us of our wrongdoing when we do what we know to be wrong. It is the judgment of conscience that so often breaks a person in the moment when facing his or her wrongdoing most directly, as when a murderer is confronted by the grief of the victim's family. In Catholic thought, the concept of conscience seems to stand in for the broader notion of human reason. Our reason is part of what signals that we have been made in the image of God. Despite the ravages of sin, it survives in the voice of conscience, which has surprisingly resilient capacities to remind us of what we know to be right and true.

A second element of the moral self is our emotions, or *passions,* best understood as the forces that incline us to act in regard to something that we believe to be good or evil. The passions are "natural components of the human psyche; they form the passageway and ensure the connection between the life of the senses and the life of the mind." Among the passions listed in Scripture are love, hatred, fear, joy, and sadness. The "heart" is described by Jesus as the center of the passions and therefore, in a sense, the center of moral life (Mark 7:21).

Moral thinkers like Plato and the Stoics warned of the dangers of the passions and sought to burn them right out of the moral life. They thought that reason must prevail, not passion. But this turns us into less than fully human aliens like the *Star Trek* character Spock. Aristotle did better in recognizing that passions themselves are an important, even indispensable, part of human nature. The issue is not whether to have passions or whether they are good but whether they are rightly felt, harnessed, and directed. Following in the tradition of Aristotle, the catechism describes the passions as morally neutral, neither good nor bad. "Passions are morally good when they contribute to a good action, evil in the opposite case." Growth toward moral goodness involves getting our passions engaged with our reason and our will so they do not rage out of control; directing them toward good ends, in keeping with God's will; and ultimately integrating them as part of the whole created self that we offer back to God in joyful service.

I discovered many good examples of the positive role of the passions when I studied Christians who rescued Jews during the Holocaust. A passionate response to the suffering they saw in the Jewish refugees who came their way motivated a large number of rescuers to risk everything to offer hospitality to these needy strangers. Moved by compassion, aching with pain at the misery of hunted women and children, of the old and the sick, rescuers acted to save lives. In many cases, passions overcame the cool counsel of reason and the dictates of caution; it was passion, far more than any other factor, that got their wills engaged to do the right thing.[8]

Closely connected with our conscience and our passions, our *character traits* constitute a third element of the moral self. The catechism says that a character trait is a "habitual and firm disposition" of our will. Elements of character include our attitudes, our intentions, our motives, and our perceptions. These aspects of our character are clearly revealed by our habitual actions and practices. For example, people who behave in a greedy fashion do so on the basis of attitudes, intentions, motives, and perceptions that come to crystallize greed as an aspect of their character. The word *character* comes from the Greek *charakter,* which was an engraving tool or the distinctive mark made by one. Just as you knew that the material was from this particular person due to the *charakter* stamped on it, so we know ourselves and especially other people by their characteristic way of being and acting in life.[9]

Character traits can take the form of virtues and vices. "A virtue is a habitual and firm disposition to do the good," says the catechism, while a vice is a habitual and firm disposition to do the evil in some area or another of life. Because the moral life has many components and there are a wide range of habits, choices, and attitudes, we are quite likely to be deficient in some virtues and strong in others. A virtuous person pursues the good with all his or her power, making good and right choices and exhibiting those good choices in concrete actions. That person is not perfect, simply virtuous. Someone who pursues vice is, similarly, *vicious*—that's where that important word came from.

So what set of steps or actions enables us to be virtuous or conscientious or rightly passionate? Culling through the catechism, the most important points are these:

• We acquire moral virtues, rightly ordered passions, and a well-functioning conscience through human effort, though such efforts are always aided by God's grace and ultimately dependent on it. Still, we cannot slough off responsibility for our proper moral development on God. *The way you become a good person is by working hard at it.*

• Right attitudes, dispositions, perceptions, and motives both create the conditions for making good choices and also are the fruits of good choices. There is a kind of moral feedback loop functioning here. *The way you become a good person is by making good choices.* This pattern of making right choices trains your will to exercise your freedom rightly over and over again. Certainly there must be some role for that old standby, willpower, in getting this ball rolling—it helps us make a choice that doesn't come naturally at first but will eventually be easy if we do it enough times. As we deliberately choose the good while being fully aware that we could choose otherwise, we grow in goodness.

• "The education of the conscience [and the passions and the virtues] is a lifelong task." *The way you become a good person is by training and educating yourself in goodness.* As a child, others train us. If we are fortunate, parents, teachers, and other people teach us what a good conscience, good use of passions, and good character look like. As an adult, we continue this education by our own choices—in churchgoing, selecting reading and entertainment, and so on.

• "The moral virtues grow through . . . perseverance in struggle." The will and ability to persevere are central to growth in moral goodness. Perseverance involves the determination to resist temptations, the fortitude to continue despite setbacks, and the generally purifying impact of the various forms of suffering that come upon us in this life. A secret of success and growth in life appears to be to welcome times of struggle and suffering as occasions for exponential growth in character. *The way you become a good person is by persevering in struggle and thus growing in virtue.*

• Spiritual progress comes through steady spiritual practices. The Christian tradition has a long history of spiritual practices that help believers grow in discipline and self-mastery. These include various forms of prayer and other practices such as meditation, fasting, pilgrimages, and silent retreats. Although some of these have certainly been taken to extremes by overzealous believers, Christians believe that the will is trained through practices involving self-discipline and occasional periods of self-denial. Therefore, *the way you become a good person is by practicing spiritual disciplines that grow your self-discipline.*

• "Christ's gift of salvation offers us the grace necessary to persevere in the pursuit of the virtues." Finally it comes down to grace. The Scriptures are abundant with various ways of describing how grace actually works in our lives. The Bible says that believers are, in a way, adopted into God's family, and so, in a sense, we get the "inheritance" of our Father's moral goodness. We are in Christ and so his life becomes our life. Christ's Spirit is in us and so he takes control of our will and our decisions. Christ remakes the image of God in humanity so that we can become the image of Christ and thus be restored to our original beauty and nobility. Christ has set us free from sin and its power and thus we are free at last. In short, *the way you become a good person is by giving your whole self over to Jesus Christ and letting him change you.*

It really is possible to become a truly good person through a process of gradual transformation in Jesus Christ. We need not accept the way we are. We can do better, with God's help and our own effort. The Christian tradition has charted the way forward. It includes forgiveness, moral effort, and moments of conversion but goes beyond these as well, into a disciplined life of moral growth and change.

In the next chapter, we will consider yet another possibility—that we might want to aspire on our life's journey not just to moral goodness but to moral *greatness.* We will consider the lives of some people who got there and ask whether we are interested in joining them.

7

What Does Moral Greatness Look Like?

Whoever wishes to become great among you
must be your servant, and whoever wishes to
be first among you must be slave of all. For the
Son of Man came not to be served but to serve,
and to give his life a ransom for many.

—Mark 10:43–45

The business writer and researcher Jim Collins has written a popular book about organizational success called *Good to Great* in which he analyzes companies along several dimensions to determine what sets the truly stellar apart from the ones that achieve adequate but unimpressive growth and success.[1] He comes up with five qualities that separate the great companies from the good ones, and hundreds of thousands of people have bought his book because they want to know how to be great. Nobody would buy a book that told them how to just get by.

In this chapter, we will do the same thing. As the saying goes in baseball, we will swing for the fences. We will not just be thinking about how a person becomes a basic, decent, garden-variety good person in life's journey. Heaven knows we need more such people. But this chapter is written out of my suspicion that many of us are interested in something more. We don't just want to be a "pretty good person," as the theologian Lewis Smedes put it.[2] We want—or are open to wanting—a more profound, richer, and more fulfilling life. Maybe we aspire to moral greatness. Maybe we think we dare not aspire to such heights, but we are certainly inspired when we see that others have scaled the moral mountaintops. This is a chapter about how human beings can go from moral goodness to moral greatness, about what real human wholeness looks like, the finest destination we can seek.

Because the whole notion of a morally great life is pretty much uncharted territory for most of us, we need real-life, flesh-and-blood guides to help us find our way. So that is how we will proceed in this chapter, taking up the stories of William Wilberforce and Florence Nightingale of England, Dietrich Bonhoeffer of Germany, and Martin Luther King Jr. of the United States. Once we have looked at their lives, we will step back and try to find some common threads that help us see more clearly what contributes to a life of moral greatness.

WILLIAM WILBERFORCE
(1759–1833): "GOD'S POLITICIAN"

William Wilberforce was the first son and namesake of a wealthy and influential merchant in the port city of Hull, in northeastern England. It would be easy to say that young William was born into privilege, and in terms of money he was, but it came in part as a result of losing his father when he was just nine years old. The money he inherited was cold comfort when his mother sent him to live with an aunt and uncle in London and to be educated at a boarding school nearby.

In London, William was exposed to a vibrant Christian faith that contrasted with his mother's nominal Anglicanism (Church of England). The influential preacher George Whitefield was in his heyday at this time, and his version of evangelical Christianity (dubbed Methodism for its methodical approach to studying Scripture) resonated deeply with the young man. Indeed, William's growing evangelical fervor disturbed his mother, who did not want her son to turn out to be what we would today call a fundamentalist. She snatched him back home just a few years later and sought to involve him in the social whirl of Hull's upper crust—and to dull his religious sensibilities. Wilberforce himself later generously concluded that the combination of his mother's worldly, party-going sensibility and his aunt and uncle's serious Methodism coalesced to help make him the man he later became: socially adept but morally and religiously serious. Still, his teenage years were unhappy, torn between two families and two very different visions of the good life.

At seventeen, Wilberforce entered Cambridge University, where the children of the elite went to school, taking it seriously only if they were so inclined. Wilberforce was not much inclined, and he remembered his college years primarily for partying, gambling, singing, dancing, drinking, and theatergoing with friends—some of whom turned out to be quite influential, including the future prime minister William Pitt. By the time he finished school, Wilberforce's faith had faded to little more than a broad moral outlook.

Upon leaving Cambridge, Wilberforce was elected to Parliament at a mere twenty-one years of age, but without a particular sense of purpose. It may be hard for us to believe that someone that young could just drift into high office, but this was possible at that time for children of privilege, who could essentially buy their parliamentary seats. Four years later, while traveling in Europe, Wilberforce experienced a fresh religious awakening. He described it as a conversion, and through it, he said, he found his purpose in life.

In 1784, looking back on his brief existence, the newly converted twenty-five-year-old felt a deep sense of remorse about his various sins and, more deeply, about his purposeless life up to that point. Ablaze with a fresh sense of passion for God and for life, he seriously considered abandoning politics and worldly affairs because of the moral challenges and compromises that such a life requires. However, with wise counsel from such influential friends as the hymn writer John Newton (the author of "Amazing Grace"), he concluded that God had placed him in politics to make a difference there. Instead of withdrawing from public life in order to retain his moral purity, he decided he would take all of his privileges, gifts, and skills and use them for the common good as a legislator. He pledged himself to finding a morally worthy cause, or set of causes, in which to invest his life and exert his worldly power. Thus he came to see his vocation in such a way that he would eventually come to be known as "God's politician."[3]

Shortly thereafter, Wilberforce became involved in the antislavery fight in Britain. At first, he had no particular personal experience or stake in the slavery issue, but when he was presented with clear and convincing evidence of the great evils of the slave trade and of slavery itself, he made its abolition his life's work. He gave his first antislavery speech in Parliament—a most impressive oratorical event, by all accounts—in 1789. Reading the text of this speech more than two centuries later, one senses the passion of a man who has found his purpose:

> There is a principle above everything that is politic, and
> when I reflect on the command which says, "Thou shalt
> do no murder," believing its authority to be divine, how
> can I dare to set up any reasonings of my own against it?
> . . . The nature and all the circumstances of this Trade are
> now laid open to us. We can no longer plead ignorance.
> We cannot evade it. We may spurn it. We may kick it out
> of the way. But we cannot turn aside so as to avoid
> seeing it. . . . This House must decide and must justify to
> all the world and to its own conscience, the rectitude of
> the grounds of its decision. . . . Let not Parliament be the
> only body that is insensible to the principles of natural
> justice.[4]

It took eighteen years of relentless parliamentary struggle to win the abolition of the slave trade in Britain, and then
for several years Wilberforce monitored events to be sure that
this abolition was enforced. It was not until 1823, another
sixteen years later, that Wilberforce and friends decided it was
time to make the next move and attack slavery itself. He initiated a campaign for the full emancipation of all of the slaves
in any region controlled by the United Kingdom. Though ill
health forced him to retire in 1825, his cause finally suc-
ceeded in 1833, just days before his death. The significance of
this feat is all the more obvious when we compare events in
England and the United States, where it took a bloody war
thirty years later to resolve the slavery issue. One commentator described the significance of the antislavery efforts of
Wilberforce and his colleagues in this way: "The unweary,
unostentatious, and inglorious crusade of England against
slavery may probably be regarded as among the three or four
perfectly virtuous pages comprised in the history of nations."[5]

Reading about Wilberforce during these years of the
antislavery struggle is deeply inspiring. I picture him as a

short, half-blind, hunched-over, unprepossessing man seated at a big conference table with his fellow reformers, studying reports on the horrible conditions on slave-trading ships and on the plantations in the British West Indies. I envision his outraged face as he brilliantly, passionately, and devotedly details these conditions to skeptical audiences in Parliament. I imagine listening as he combats the cynics and opportunists who appeal to Britain's financial self-interest and make fallacious arguments about how slavery is not so bad after all, at least for black Africans who don't know any better. I watch him as he argues forcefully but respectfully behind closed doors with his longtime friend, the prime minister, William Pitt, trying to get him to support the abolitionist side without destroying their important working friendship. I think about the many incidents in which he is attacked in the press, physically threatened by those whose interests he is challenging, and tempted by the worldly rewards that could have been his had he been willing to abandon his quest to abolish slavery.

> *Wilberforce became the first politician to embody a type of character that became important in all modern democracies: the morally serious statesman who puts doing the right thing above personal ambition or partisan advance.*

Wilberforce became the first politician to embody a type of character that became important in all modern democracies: the morally serious statesman who puts doing the right thing above personal ambition or partisan advance, who uses his power to advance the cause of "the least of these," whose moral nobility raises the bar for all others who hold high office. Our appreciation for Wilberforce only grows when we consider his relentless work for other causes, some of which he began to tackle as early as 1787: reforming church, prison, and labor laws; imposing limits on the death penalty; ending flogging in the military; suppressing animal cruelty; protecting Indians under British rule; advancing education for the poor; and helping establish Sierra Leone as a haven for freed slaves. Wilberforce was involved in more than sixty social and philanthropic agencies attempting to make Great Britain and all of its colonies and territories more humane and more Christian, in the best sense. His example helped inspire the formation of countless other societies, charities, and similar efforts.

At the time of his death, Wilberforce was celebrated for his impact on Great Britain. His tombstone in Westminster Abbey bears the following words:

> Eminent as he was in every department of public labour,
> and a leader in every work of charity, whether to relieve
> the temporal or the spiritual wants of his fellow men,
> his name will ever be specially identified with those
> exertions, which, by the blessing of God, removed from
> England the guilt of the African slave trade, and prepared
> the way for the abolition of slavery in every colony of
> the empire.

FLORENCE NIGHTINGALE (1820–1910): FIGHTING FOR HEALTH AND FOR WOMEN

Florence Nightingale was born to a family of considerable wealth, even more wealth than William Wilberforce had enjoyed. Her father, William Nightingale, was a man of leisure who devoted some of his resources to the needy while also taking much time to teach his precocious daughter, Florence, who became one of the most highly educated women in England. The family enjoyed all of the comforts money could buy—servants, multiple homes and constant travel between them, European vacations, nearly infinite leisure time, and every other nicety of upper-class life. The family's religious life is described differently in different sources; despite the Nightingales' involvement in the Anglican church, a significant strand of unconventional religious thinking apparently ran through the family, especially in the views of William, a Unitarian. The patriarch, and later his daughter, embraced a theologically unorthodox but apparently a highly motivating Christian spirituality that emphasized making the most of your life on this earth for some worthy cause.

It is clear that from an early age, Florence Nightingale dreaded the concept of growing up to a life of sitting around sipping tea at boring parties and being the quiet consort to a dominant husband. She wrote, "A woman cannot live in the light of intellect. Society forbids it. Those conventional frivolities which are called her duties forbid it. Her domestic duties, high sounding words which for the most part are bad habits . . . forbid it."[6] She burned with the desire for an active life, a life that mattered, a life for God, and after a mystical experience at the age of sixteen, she was convinced that God had spoken to her and called her to some special work.[7] Soon enough that calling was clarified as a life in nursing, though her vision always extended further. From her parents' perspective, nursing was an appalling choice, the province of drunks and lowlifes, but for Florence it became the object of her determined commitment. She had several serious suitors but put away all ideas of marriage by the time she reached thirty and never looked back from her determined pursuit of the kind of meaningful professional life routinely denied to women at this time in history. In this pursuit, she was influenced by the example of women such as Elizabeth Fry and Hannah Nicholson, both of whom were independent-minded social reformers already at work in England.

After three years of nursing training and early service as a nurse director in the 1850s, the Crimean War—aptly described by one observer as "one of history's most useless wars"—proved to be the momentous cause that Florence Nightingale had been waiting for. The British military had proved appallingly unprepared for dealing with the casualties of this now obscure war among England, France, Turkey, and Russia, and its cry for medical help from back home inspired Nightingale to respond. In an unprecedented role for a woman, Nightingale was quickly named chief nurse of the Barrack Hospital in the war zone. When she arrived to take charge, she was nauseated and enraged at the horrendous, chaotic conditions there, which caused the unnecessary deaths of hundreds of soldiers.

Nightingale rolled up her sleeves and got to work, not just offering nursing services but reorganizing the entire system of care for wounded soldiers. This meant that there was no aspect of the lives of these soldiers and their caregivers that she did not address: the provision of food, medicine, and other supplies; laundry services; education; entertainment; hygiene; doctor training; statistical analysis of mortality and recovery rates; and a range of other efforts accompanying the normal grind of attempting to save the lives of men who had been wounded in battle. She herself did battle with the authorities as she sought to bend the entire military apparatus to her will, at least as it related to meeting the needs of wounded soldiers. Nightingale is often misunderstood as "merely" the saintly "lady of the lamp," in the words of Henry Wadsworth Longfellow's tribute. Yes, certainly, she worked tirelessly, tending to her patients and supervising their care. But her moral greatness is best understood when the whole picture is considered: serving in a dangerous and highly infectious medical environment, battling with recalcitrant government and military officials, spending her own money to meet the needs of her troops when the government failed to do what was needed, writing fundraising letters to get the funds to meet other needs, traveling between hospitals in a dangerous war zone, skipping meals and nights of sleep as she worked around the clock, and much more. Under her leadership, the mortality rate for injured soldiers dropped dramatically.

Upon returning to England, Nightingale threw herself into a wide variety of very intense efforts to study the disastrous British experience in the Crimea and to see that changes were made to prevent the same situation from happening again. She instituted reforms in military medicine and associated military practices, functioning as what one observer called the "stealth Secretary of War," despite the continued opposition of military leaders. She had no official position besides serving on study commissions and writing various reports, but her moral influence and relentless efforts were too great to be ignored. (Her warm relationship with Queen Victoria didn't hurt, either.) When she spoke or wrote about an issue, she was always extremely well prepared and always positioned on the moral high ground, fighting selflessly and without personal reward for the well-being of people who needed an advocate.

Besides her efforts related to medical care in the military, Nightingale initiated reforms in hospitals and hospital construction practices, promoted the establishment of health care in the wretched English workhouses for the poor (as well as other efforts on behalf of the poor), advanced public health through the East London Nursing Society, reformed army practices in India related to health, wrote the key text-book in nurse training, and founded two nurse-training schools. She is rightly recognized as the founder and patron saint of the modern nursing profession.

Where was Florence Nightingale's religious faith in her tireless efforts? Some biographies have tried to make her out to be a saintly evangelical Christian. She may have been saintly— I guess that's what this chapter is attempting to suggest—but it was not a conventional Christian piety that motivated her.

A closer look at her many religious writings reveals that Nightingale was a believer in God who cannot be said to have embraced orthodox Christianity. She was a serious religious thinker in her own right and spent many years working on what amounted to a rethinking of Christian faith. Her book, published in 1859 under the title *Suggestions for Thought to the Searchers After Truth,* reveals that she was quite a radical thinker.[8] She rejected biblical or church authority and did not accept the belief that Jesus is the only Savior ever to appear in human history. She despised any emphasis on heaven or future life and its rewards. One commentator writes, "Nightingale had little patience with theologies that centered on a future life. Her . . . passions . . . were all centred in a belief in the capacity of the individual human being. She was interested in this earth, the people on it, and the possibility of creating a just society where [all] people were able to develop their particular gifts."[9] Nightingale believed that faith was about moving toward personal moral perfection and especially the improvement of this world through hard work and concrete actions.

Her moral thinking had a strong feminist streak, and she was especially interested in opening up society for women to have as many opportunities as possible. She wanted to "strive after a better life for women."[10]

It turns out, then, that Florence Nightingale actually pursued at least a two-track strategy. Her public work primarily involved advancing health care, especially the nursing profession and its practice. But she was also very much driven by a desire to open doors for women and was aware that everything that she did as a first for a woman itself contributed to opening those doors. Both tracks of her life's work were motivated by her unconventional but deeply held faith and her strong sense of a mystical divine calling from an early age. This was Florence Nightingale's version of moral greatness, and its impact continues to be felt around the world.

DIETRICH BONHOEFFER (1906–1945): THEOLOGIAN AND RESISTER

Like Wilberforce and Nightingale, Dietrich Bonhoeffer was favorably born. He was the sixth of eight children in a cultured German family whose head was Karl Bonhoeffer, one of the leading psychiatrists and scholars in Germany at the turn of the twentieth century. Both Karl and Dietrich's mother, Paula, were talented, intelligent, and demanding people who nurtured and expected only the best from their children.[11]

Young Dietrich was a pensive and sensitive child, more religiously disposed than his scientifically inclined father. His introspection was deepened when he lost his brother Walter during World War I, and he went on to study theology at

Tübingen and in Berlin. As a precocious twenty-one-year-old, Bonhoeffer completed his first dissertation while also qualifying for licensure as a Lutheran minister. Just three years later, at twenty-four, he completed his second thesis, and not long after, in 1930, he began what looked like a very promising career as a theologian at the University of Berlin.

History intervened, however. In 1933, the Nazis came to power in Germany and quickly set about their totalitarian project of gaining control over all aspects of German society. The Bonhoeffer family, solidly anti-Nazi from the very beginning, recognized Hitler's aggressive national renewal based on blood, violence, and race as both immoral and ultimately disastrous. Germany had fallen into the hands of gangsters, and the Bonhoeffers knew it.

In Germany at that time, both university service and employment in the church required government approval in one form or another, because both were in effect agencies of the government. Hitler's minions tightened the reins on Germany's scholars and worked to do the same with Germany's Protestant ministers. No committed anti-Nazi lasted long in university life during those years, and Bonhoeffer was no exception. He left his post at the University of Berlin in October 1933 and took a leadership role in the anti-Nazi opposition at a time when German Protestant churches were increasingly susceptible to Nazi racism in thought and practice.

Bonhoeffer was among the most radical voices in German Christianity during the period from 1933 to 1939. He opposed Nazi meddling in church life, expressed concern about Nazi anti-Semitism, led an underground seminary that sought to train ministers who would resist the nazification of the church, wrote books and essays that clearly but carefully articulated an alternative moral vision to the one spreading in

Germany, participated in international ecumenical conferences and peace efforts, and finally left Germany in the summer of 1939 to enter what looked like a long period of exile in America. But he didn't stay.

The many elite Germans (including the prominent theologians Karl Barth, who went to Switzerland, and Paul Tillich, who settled in the United States and taught at both Union Theological Seminary and Harvard University) who left their country at this time enjoyed long and prosperous careers abroad. The theologian John de Gruchy wrote that if Bonhoeffer had stayed in America, "he might have dominated the theological scene in the second half of the twentieth century."[12] One can only wonder with melancholic sadness about the books that he might have produced if he had had thirty more years of productive labor.

But this is where Bonhoeffer's moral greatness really begins to become apparent: Bonhoeffer took, quite literally, the last ship back to Germany right before Hitler's invasion of Poland and the beginning of World War II. In a farewell letter to his Union Seminary colleague Reinhold Niebuhr, Bonhoeffer wrote, "I have made a mistake in coming to America. I must live through this difficult period of our national history with the Christian people of Germany. I will have no right to participate in the reconstruction of Christian life in Germany after the war if I do not share in the trials of this time with my people."[13]

It is not just that Bonhoeffer went back to Germany. He went back with the express intent of resisting Hitler in every way he could. Because every able-bodied man in Germany had to play some role in the war effort, he worked to get himself placed in a military counterintelligence unit that was a beehive of resistance to Hitler. The articulate, open resistance of his earlier years now gave way to a stealthy and dangerous life as a double agent. Eventually, this group of conspirators became involved in a plot to assassinate Hitler.

It was probably only a matter of time before this circle of resisters was discovered. Bonhoeffer was arrested in April 1943 and languished in prison for two full years until he was finally executed on Hitler's personal order on April 9, 1945, along with several others in his resistance group, including members of the Bonhoeffer family. The war in Europe ended just four weeks later. Hitler himself was dead by the end of April. Bonhoeffer was among the last of this evil man's millions of victims.

Every generation produces a small number of truly outstanding thinkers in various fields, and Bonhoeffer had enough time in the early stages of his career to write several books that continue to be studied with deep appreciation today. For example, his book *The Cost of Discipleship* remains a favorite for its piercing account of the moral demands of authentic Christian faith. His collected *Letters and Papers from Prison* offer a moving look at his developing thought and his difficult experiences under imprisonment. *Ethics,* also drafted during this period, remains an important, though fragmentary, treatment of the moral dimension of the Christian faith.[14]

But what moves Bonhoeffer from just another great thinker to moral hero, in my view, is his combination of moral discernment, courage, and sacrifice. In a time when millions of his fellow German Christians saw Adolf Hitler as a national savior sent by God, Bonhoeffer saw him for the wretched tyrant that he was. In a time when millions were being sucked into what became a lethal hatred of Jews, Bonhoeffer saw that anti-Semitism was an evil that violates all biblical principles. In a time when Hitler and others played the patriotism card to demand loyal obedience to the Nazi German vision, Bonhoeffer discerned that true patriotism required resistance, not obedience.

But without moral courage, moral discernment reduces to simply having the right opinion. Courage involves living out the implications of what you discern, which is exactly what Bonhoeffer did from the very beginning of the Nazi era. He could have compromised with Nazism to stay in his teaching and church posts. Countless other people did; Bonhoeffer did not. He could have fled to Switzerland or America or many other places. That would have been discerning. But it would not have been as courageous as returning to Germany to fight the evil that was enthroned there. He could have come back to Germany and used his family influence to find a fairly safe post in which he could survive the war. But instead he got himself right in the middle of a conspiracy against one of the most evil men ever to rule a country. In doing so, he actually sacrificed not only his personal comfort and then his freedom and finally his life but also the moral clarity that goes with perfect consistency.

> *Courage involves living out the implications of what you discern, which is exactly what Bonhoeffer did from the very beginning of the Nazi era.*

What I mean is this: Bonhoeffer did not find it easy to justify even an indirect connection with a scheme to murder Hitler. It would have been easier to keep "clean hands," as he himself reflected while he was in prison. Many anti-Nazi Christians believed that quiet opposition confined to prayer, unsullied by worldly resistance activities, was preferable to the alternative. But Bonhoeffer concluded that it was morally wrong to keep clean hands, to remain pure and unsullied in a context that is bathed in the blood of innocent victims. In this sense, a pure conscience and clean hands are a luxury bought at the expense of other people's suffering. What makes Bonhoeffer morally great is that he sacrificed everything, including his clean hands, in order to act responsibly—as he understood what that meant in his situation. It was the culminating act of a life in which responsibility—for Germany, for Christian integrity, for innocent victims of tyranny—governed Bonhoeffer's choices. It ended up costing him his life, leaving Bonhoeffer as a strangely modern kind of martyr, killed not for believing in Jesus but for understanding that belief in Jesus required a dramatic act of political resistance in a context of grave evil.

In one of his last compositions, while in prison, Bonhoeffer wrote a poem, "Stations on the Road to Freedom," that aptly summarizes the journey to moral greatness. Here is part of it:

> Daring to do what is right, not what fancy
>   may tell you,
> valiantly grasping occasions, not cravenly
>   doubting—
> freedom comes only through deeds, not
>   through thoughts taking wing.
> Faint not nor fear, but go out to the storm
>   and the action,
> trusting in God whose commandment you
>   faithfully follow;
> freedom, exultant, will welcome your spirit
>   with joy.[15]

MARTIN LUTHER KING JR. (1929–1968): LEADER OF A PEOPLE'S STRUGGLE FOR LIBERATION

In retrospect, it is easy to see that Martin Luther King Jr. was perfectly positioned to lead black Americans in their struggle for a decent and dignified life. Born and raised in Atlanta, King was the son and grandson of influential Baptist pastors, both of whom, in succession, led the important Ebenezer Baptist Church.

Southern black communities have long had an internal life, including their churches, of which whites are largely unaware. One aspect of that inner life has traditionally been the role played by pastors who have served as their people's advocates, defenders, and encouragers in dealing with the injustices of a white-dominated society. King grew up watching both his father and grandfather stand firm against white racism while also hearing them preach a message of empowerment and self-reliance for the black community. Thus the message was double-edged: we will stand up for you and fight for justice against white racism *and* we will demand that you make the most of whatever opportunities are available to you. Both aspects of this message were rooted in an understanding of the Christian faith, which says that God requires both resistance to injustice and personal responsibility from his people. This message was proclaimed with passion both in the pulpit and around the dinner table.

King was clearly a brilliant young man. He quickly proceeded through his education, graduating from a (segregated) high school at fifteen and from historically all-black Morehouse College at nineteen. At this stage of his life, he made the fateful choice to leave the South and segregated schools and go to the North for college and eventually for his seminary and doctoral training. He earned a ministry degree at the interdenominational Crozer Seminary in Pennsylvania and a doctorate in theology at Boston University. When he finished his academic work, in 1954, he was just twenty-five years old.

A voracious learner, King mastered the (white) Western theological and ethical tradition. He was also deeply influenced by his reading of Gandhi, the nonviolent liberator of the Indian people from British rule. His encyclopedic memory allowed him to retain whatever he read. With this body of knowledge, combined with his moral passion and his brilliance as a preacher (both as a personal gift and as a legacy of the black church tradition), King was able to communicate effectively with both white and black audiences—quoting Scripture and philosophy and employing the rhetoric that was most appropriate to his setting. Like most leaders of minority groups, King was, in effect, bilingual and bicultural, able to cross cultural and linguistic barriers and move with ease in both the minority and majority cultures.

King might have used these gifts for just about any purpose. He could have gotten rich in business. He could have settled into an academic life in either a "white" or "black" setting. Or he could have quietly pastored a church, perhaps in a region of the North or West where the raw racism of the South was not as great a factor. He certainly considered doing so.

Instead, in 1954, King and his wife, Coretta, made the conscious decision to take a pastorate in the heart of Dixie: Montgomery, Alabama. He had been there just eighteen months when Rosa Parks made her famous decision to refuse to give up her seat to a white man and move to the back of the bus. King did not seek the leadership of what became the Montgomery bus boycott; he was selected for it by fellow pastors and black community leaders. For his first speech in this role, delivered on December 5, 1955, he had just a few minutes to prepare. This speech, offered to a packed house at Holt Street Baptist Church in Montgomery, publicly launched the boycott. Eventually his leadership of the boycott led to his national recognition.

The rest of the story is well known. The yearlong Montgomery bus boycott ended in success after the Supreme Court ruled that bus segregation was unconstitutional. The nonviolent protest model employed in Montgomery soon spread across the South, because of course it wasn't only Montgomery that segregated its public facilities, its public schools, and its public spaces.

In September 1958, the previously ad hoc movement for black civil rights took institutional form with the founding of the Southern Christian Leadership Conference (SCLC) under King's leadership. This group, along with (and sometimes in tension with) long-established black empowerment organizations like the National Association for the Advancement of Colored People (NAACP) and the Urban League, now led a direct assault on the centuries-old systemic dehumanization, disenfranchisement, and discrimination to which black Americans were subjected. For the next ten years, King traversed the country—primarily the South but also Chicago and other northern cities—leading campaigns to remove various forms of discrimination in one city after another.

Images from those years still linger in the American memory, as well they should: the firehoses and police dogs being turned on black marchers in Birmingham; the majestic March on Washington and "I Have a Dream" speech in 1963; the signing of the Civil Rights Act of 1964 and the

Voting Rights Act of 1965; and the worst of all, the picture of King lying bleeding on the balcony of the Lorraine Motel on April 4, 1968, after his assassination. Those not very familiar with King's life may mistakenly conclude that his assassination was an unexpected and tragic shock. Unfortunately, this was not the case. King was the object of death threats and actual acts of violence repeatedly from the moment that he took leadership in the civil rights movement. His home was bombed more than once. He received hundreds of hate-filled letters each week. His family was threatened. He was stabbed in New York in 1958. Crowds attacked and beat him in several cities. He had rocks thrown at him. He was imprisoned numerous times for minor infractions.

One aspect of moral greatness is sheer physical courage. It is not always required, but courage in the face of violence is usually a part of any work that involves challenging social injustice. Such courage does not come naturally to anyone, and it does not come without a struggle. One of King's biographers, Stephen Oates, tells a critically important story from the Montgomery days, in which King faced not just the threat but the likelihood of his own death and had to decide whether to proceed with the work. After receiving a death threat over the phone late one night, King felt tempted to give up:

> He put his head in his hands and bowed over the table. "Oh, Lord," he prayed aloud. "I'm down here trying to do what is right. But, Lord, I must confess that I'm weak now. I'm afraid. The people are looking to me for leadership, and if I stand before them without strength and courage, they too will falter. I am at the end of my powers. I have nothing left. I can't face it alone." He sat there, his head still bowed in his hands, tears burning his

eyes. But then he felt something—a presence, a stirring
in himself. And it seemed that an inner voice was
speaking to him with quiet assurance: "Martin Luther,
stand up for righteousness. Stand up for justice. Stand up
for truth. And, lo, I will be with you, even unto the end
of the world."[16]

King's faith clearly sustained him in the most profound
manner imaginable at this moment of crisis. His living relationship with God nurtured him, as did his knowledge of the
Scriptures and the testimony of those who had suffered for
doing right, including Jesus himself.

But King brought more to the table than his faith. He
also brought a finely honed mind, which included a theoret-
ical framework for understanding the reality of his situation,
the way it needed to be changed, and the costs that would be
incurred in changing it. King analyzed the black situation in
America as systemic structural injustice. Slavery had been fol-
lowed by segregation for blacks, and an American form of
apartheid had developed in large parts of the country. This
system benefited whites, and it was undergirded by centuries
of misinformation and miseducation about the supposed natural inferiority of blacks. Bad ideas rooted in a bad system, a
bad system bringing benefits to some at the expense of
others, millions of otherwise decent, well-intended white
folks caught up in this systemic evil—King saw that such a
reality would last more or less forever unless it was confronted directly.

King was not alone in his view that structural racism is
evil and must be confronted unswervingly. But his unique
contribution was to attack systemic racism with a strategy of
nonviolent direct action. His plan was to recruit millions of

black foot soldiers (and a few brave white partners) to throw their bodies at the most visible symbols of this racism—at segregated lunch counters, buses, restaurants, schools, and neighborhoods. They knew that such actions would undoubtedly elicit a violent response but believed that if the movement retained its disciplined nonviolence, they could take the moral high ground. They would eventually prevail, not just because they would win the battle for public opinion (which they would) but also because their cause was right. King loved to say that "the arc of the universe bends toward justice." Justice may not come immediately, but it will come one day—if people fight for it using the weapons of the spirit rather than the flesh. The unjust suffering that marchers and other participants in the movement bore would ultimately be redemptive, just as Jesus' unjust suffering was redemptive. It was as if the movement could drain the swamp of structural racism only by absorbing its poison themselves. They would have to suffer to win liberation. And King, as the leader of this movement, would have to endure a large number of these blows personally. He took the ultimate blow with his assassination, but after 350 years, the power of systemic, legalized discrimination against blacks in America had been broken.

> *The unjust suffering that marchers and other participants in the [civil rights] movement bore would ultimately be redemptive, just as Jesus' unjust suffering was redemptive.*

THE INGREDIENTS OF
MORAL GREATNESS

Moral heroes are not superhuman. As we consider the lives of people like Wilberforce, Nightingale, Bonhoeffer, and King, it's important to remember that these are recognizably human persons, flawed and fallible, just like us. We haven't lingered over these flaws, but they were there.

There are certain native advantages in the four people we have discussed here. All came from positions of at least relative privilege. All were clearly blessed with strong intelligence. All were well educated, though of course that involves hard work and not just giftedness. All were brilliant communicators. These gifts, too, of course, were honed by practice and hard work.

So we might conclude that unless we are privileged, intelligent, well educated, skillful communicators we cannot aspire to moral greatness. Of course, that is not the whole story. All of these moral leaders dealt with frustration and suffering in their early years, and each found a way to make constructive use of that suffering in deepening their compassion for others and in broadening and strengthening their faith, personalities, and moral commitments. All these leaders exercised wise discernment and found a moral purpose at a pivotal moment in their lives and then proceeded to give their lives to that purpose. Each had a passion to accomplish some morally profound goal that was the animating center of their lives. In each case, they were ahead of their peers in seeing the moral reality of their situation for what it was.

It was inevitable that all of them faced resistance in pursuing their goals. All faced fierce criticism and physical threats. Besides the verbal critiques, Wilberforce was threatened physically, Nightingale faced daily risks and essentially ruined her health, and both Bonhoeffer and King were im-prisoned and eventually mur-dered. In dealing with criticism, hatred, risk, and danger, each leader made the decision to pro-ceed with his or her work. All were relentless in pursuing their moral passions. This relentlessness and commitment made each of them seem like radicals to many of their contemporaries. Perhaps the lesson here is that the judg-ment of the average morally mediocre contemporary is not a good plumb line for assessing our own behavior.

> *Perhaps the lesson here is that the judgment of the average morally mediocre contemporary is not a good plumb line for assessing our own behavior.*

All four leaders gathered around themselves a team of like-minded partners. In lifting up the lives of individual moral leaders, it is easy to overlook those who worked with them—Wilberforce and Nightingale both had reformist col-leagues scattered throughout England; Bonhoeffer had broth-ers and sisters in the resistant church and stealthy colleagues in the political resistance; King had an entire civil rights move-ment and many fellow religious and civic leaders. Together, these teams of people helped these moral leaders analyze sit-uations, plan strategy, communicate their shared vision, and stay the course.

Perhaps above all, or underneath all, each of the people profiled here was animated by religious faith. Their love for God motivated their desire to make this world a better place. Their versions of the Christian faith differed in many ways. Their spiritual practices were undoubtedly different.

But in the end, it is not too simple to say that for each, love of God motivated love of neighbor. They gave their lives to serving others because of a fundamental life commitment to serving God. This became the purpose of their life's journey, and it was in giving themselves away that they found true wholeness, true fulfillment, and true greatness.

8

Where Can True Wholeness Be Found?

Thy kingdom come, thy will be done,
on earth as it is in heaven.

— MATTHEW 6:10

During the summer of the year I turned sixteen, I embarked on an intense quest for meaning in life. My desire for more knowledge and understanding had been building for some time, but by the time I hit sixteen, my need to find meaning for myself had become more or less unbearable. After a variety of pretty pitiful attempts, involving girlfriends, the occult, UFOs, sports, and the effort to sculpt a "hot body" courtesy of the workout center (connected to the girlfriends angle), I found God. It has been quite a journey in the twenty-five years since that summer, and my understanding of what it means to have found God—or to have been found by God, which was definitely how I experienced it—has changed in many ways. But the essential task that I accomplished that summer has never had to be repeated. I found the meaning of my life and a sense of where wholeness might lie when I aligned my own personal journey and purpose with the journey and purpose of God, as understood in the Christian tradition.

I have written this book for people who have embarked on a quest for meaning and for wholeness much like mine in my sixteenth year. My goal has been to offer a gentle and accessible Christian account of how to find the answers that I was looking for that summer and that many people are looking for at any given time, all the time.

My main point of entry has been to puzzle over the question of human nature. The riddle of my own nature is part of what nearly drove me mad during the most intense period of my search. I was a smart kid, fairly athletic, from a good family. But I was miserable and angry and confused and disappointed in myself and absolutely without direction in life. I was appalled at the junk that was in me and my inability to be a better person on my own. I sensed that I had been brought into the world for a reason and that until I figured out what that reason was, I could never find peace.

> *I sensed that I had been brought into the world for a reason and that until I figured out what that reason was, I could never find peace.*

One of the best things about becoming a Christian was that I eventually gained access to an entire seemingly inexhaustible tradition engaged in thinking about such ultimate questions. At first, only a sliver of that tradition was made available to me in the fairly fundamentalist youth group and church that I attended after my conversion at sixteen. A certain version of very Protestant faith was taught there, but that community did not know much of the broad tradition of the church that we have considered in this book. One of the greatest joys of my own life's journey over these twenty-five years has been to gain access to that tradition and to become a participant in the ongoing process of learning it, reworking it, and communicating it to others.

In this book, I have tried to communicate that part of the tradition that speaks to core issues about how to find wholeness in life's journey. My assumption has been that this task cannot be accomplished without thinking about who and what we are, our nature as human beings. And so we have dug around a bit in the Christian tradition (and sometimes among its competitors), asking what insights might be available for understanding our nature.

We have considered the question of whether there is in fact a shared human nature for us to talk about and concluded that there is such a nature, even if individuals vary dramatically, even sometimes perversely. We have looked at the mysterious internal makeup of the human self, proposing that a trinitarian body, soul, and spirit model might make the most sense of the complexity and the unity of what we find when we look at ourselves.

We have reflected on the way we are embedded in relationships of all types and how significant these are in shaping our identity. We have examined the issue of human sinfulness and concluded that to call human beings "sinners" is an accurate, though not an exhaustive, way of talking about who and what we are. We have considered the question of whether we are really free and found that our freedom is elusive, fragile, limited, and yet precious. We have explored the formation of moral character, especially the intensive effort required to move character in the direction of goodness, and we have scaled the mountaintop to catch a glimpse of the possibility of moral greatness through sacrificial service to humanity.

Lurking behind our discussion of moral character is a question that we have not yet confronted directly: What exactly does wholeness look like? I have often used the image of life as a journey and have alluded to wholeness as something we are seeking. But even if our internal self is well integrated, even if our relationships are healthy, even if we are growing morally and gaining victory over sinful patterns, and even if we are serving humanity, is that all there is to say about the destination we should be seeking? Is there something else out there? To what destination are we going?

———

I hope it has been implicit throughout this book what I will now make explicit: many of the goals that people pursue as the destination of their lives are completely inadequate for the task. What a tragedy, really—to think of so many people scurrying around from day to day *pursuing something that just doesn't matter.* Pursuing wealth that cannot bring happiness and you cannot take with you. Pursuing a beautiful body even though it will age and eventually die. Pursuing power over other people, as if it could last forever. Pursuing the latest gadgets as if they can fill the emptiness inside. What a waste.

Many astute observers have noticed that as the religious and moral heritage of the West faded in the twentieth century, the worship of materialism spread. Human beings have become consumers, soulless and manipulated by market forces, spending their Sundays shopping in secular temples of commerce rather than worshiping in the sacred cathedrals left over from a more religious age.

It was more than the intellectual challenges to the Christian faith that turned cultures of worship into cultures of shopping. The rise of capitalism, with its relentless quest for new markets and its reconfiguring of society to depend on constant economic growth, has created a culture in which all of us, from our earliest days, are trained to "shop till we drop." It should come as no surprise that many of us have accepted our training as consumers, fairly oblivious to the faint impact of contrary teachings from, among other sources, religious faith.

But the mistake of establishing material possessions or other earthly treasures and pleasures as one's highest hope is nothing new. As early as Aristotle, in the fourth century BCE, one sees the patient yet firm instruction of a philosopher attempting to demonstrate the vanity and folly of a life built on the quest for anything less than the highest human good, which he understood as a rational life of virtue. He spoke with contempt of the masses who seek possessions, wealth, or pleasure as their highest attainment: "The utter servility of the masses comes out in their preference for a bovine existence."[1] Aristotle is saying, quite starkly, that the masses live like cows in their quest for pleasure, as if there were no difference between human beings and herd animals. Ecclesiastes 1:14, of course, struck these same notes even earlier in claiming that a life lived for pleasure and treasure was "vanity and a chasing after wind." There is nothing *there*, no ultimate satisfaction, and yet millions—today more than ever—live as if there were great value in the pursuit.

We dealt with this issue in Chapter Four when we considered the concept of sin as misdirected love. If we place our fondest hopes in money and the pleasures and treasures that money can buy, our loves are misdirected. One need not embrace an ascetic ethic of simplicity to ultimately recognize the futility of such a life. "He who dies with the most toys wins" is one of the most cynical philosophies of life ever articulated—and one of the most foolish. That some people articulate such hopes, and that more live accordingly, speaks volumes concerning the true shape of human nature. It shows that we are fully capable of blinding our eyes to the highest possibilities of our nature, even though in every generation and every culture, voices of wisdom point out the folly of choosing a lesser good when a greater one is available. However often the philosophers point out the vanity and folly of a life that seeks nothing more than physical and material pleasures, there will always be some among us who choose such a life anyway. The Christian account of this aspect of life—and here our tradition is not unique—acknowledges the value of the treasures and pleasures that a good God has made available to human beings, as well as the basic human need for a decent minimum of material well-being. But the tradition has also been consistent in claiming that the relentless quest for more and more material and physical pleasures is a great trap and folly and falls well short of what we should hope for if we seek wholeness in life's journey.

This book has talked quite a bit about the elements of the human person and the struggle to bring these elements into harmony. This struggle is sufficiently difficult—and success in this arena is sufficiently meaningful—that many thinkers in human history have considered a happy, well-ordered, healthy self the destination of our human strivings.

Philosophers, religious leaders, psychologists, and others have offered various proposals for bringing harmony to the different dimensions of the self. A typical proposal, first floated by Plato in the fifth century BCE, said that we can get control of our passions and desires through the strict application of reason. The self's competing parts must be brought under the subjection of reason through careful training. In the end, this triumph of reason brings a blessed order and peace to the self.

The Stoics of the first and second centuries took this emphasis on reason in a striking direction by focusing on the virtue of resignation, which meant developing a studied indifference to all that one could not control. They were saying that if we cannot make the world what we want it to be (which is true), it is best to simply resign from the effort. Serenity is gained when we stop worrying about what we cannot control. Since what we cannot control is basically everything in life other than our own will, it is only our will that we should worry about. The successful Stoic develops a well-ordered self by amputating the emotional life, renouncing an emotional response to any stimulus from outside the self. Perhaps in some cases the Stoic approach worked, but at what price? It is hard to believe that the best destination for our lives is the annihilation of our passions and emotions, the peace that flows from emotional surrender. And yet the Stoic option has had an enduring appeal, especially in hard times, when events spin out of control, suffering is great, and all that can be controlled is the self amid turmoil and desolation.

We have seen that the historic Christian tradition has its own resources for the construction of a healthy self. Several chapters have considered questions related to the makeup of the human self, the forces that disrupt internal order and peace, and the way in which the self can be trained (or retrained) to achieve virtue. The point to remember in the Christian tradition is that the composite human body-soul-spirit unity, designed by God and fundamental to every human life, has been damaged by sin in its various forms. We sense the effects of that damage every day, we feel the tear in our own nature, and we often face its tragic consequences. Every human being has the latent capacity to know, at least dimly, what a well-ordered and virtuous life looks like and has some freedom to train the self to pursue it. However, the infusion of grace that is made available to the follower of Jesus Christ, as well as the teaching resources of the faith and the model he provided, make possible a thoroughgoing reclamation of the self. We do not find perfection, but we do make progress.

It is not hard to see that a happy, well-ordered, and virtuous self, healed of its divisions and inclined toward choosing what is right, is a higher and more refined goal. And yet, contrary to the inclinations of some of the world's greatest thinkers, the Christian tradition is not yet satisfied with this. Our highest aspirations extend beyond the self.

———

The strands of human nature—our need for relationship, the way sin disrupts them, and our potential for moral greatness in demonstrating loving concern for others—could be woven together to point to the conclusion that the destination most deeply worth cherishing would be reconciled and peaceable relationships in every dimension of human existence. Martin Luther King Jr. spoke of the quest for the "beloved community," all people living in harmony with each other. This is the kind of hope I am talking about here.

Surely this vision of wholeness in human community ranks near the pinnacle of things worth striving for. We are all acutely aware of the wretchedness of broken human bonds, whether in family life, in race relations, in churches, within nations, or in the international community. And we are deeply moved by those honorable human beings, like King and others we have discussed, who give their lives to the work of human reconciliation and community building in one form or another.

Such a destination for one's life makes the pursuit of purely personal pleasure and material well-being look remarkably small and petty by comparison. Indeed, there is hardly a comparison worth making. More subtly, such an understanding of what true wholeness is also demonstrates the selfish limits of a life given to the quest for personal virtue, personal peace, or personal happiness. If life does not include a passionate concern for social peace, social order, and restored community, the goal of achieving a healthy and well-ordered self can be just a refined kind of egotism.

In comparing a life directed to the achievement of personal wholeness with one focused on reconciled relationships, we are reminded of an unfortunate tear within the Christian tradition itself. Large sectors of the Christian community articulate and reach out for the hope of personal wholeness, especially the eternal wholeness of a life in heaven with God. "If you die today, do you know that you will meet God in heaven?" This may be the most common evangelistic appeal that Christians offer. It is easy to see that even this alluring hope of eternal life and ultimate union with God, glorious and exalted as it is, remains a highly personalized vision. It is as if God's goal for the entire course of human history is nothing more than an effort to bring *personal* wholeness, healing, and eternal salvation to as many individuals as possible. This is certainly the message proclaimed in thousands of churches.

What a glorious hope this is! I want eternal life with God. Millions of believers have lived their lives with this hope as the centerpiece of their existence. But it lacks the social dimension that I have argued is so central to the entire Christian message—and so central to human nature itself. It is a vision that I believe implies an escape from the far less happy outcome that others will face. It is about *me*, not about *us*; about my salvation, not the world's. I get to go to heaven, and I leave those less fortunate, and the world itself, behind.

A better understanding of the Christian faith is that God did more than make a scattered collection of individual "*me*'s." He made a world. And he has a bigger plan than rescuing a select few out of the world and out of eternal perdition. God's project is not just the personal salvation of you and me but the redemption of the world as a whole. This leads to a different kind of proposal as to the ultimate destination of life's journey.

———

Instead of these more personal emphases, our ultimate goal should be *to contribute to the triumph of God in the world*. We should hope and work toward the day that in all things, in all aspects of life, including human life, including our own particular lives, God will prevail. What God wants to happen on earth is what actually happens. No more violence; no more sorrow; no more victimization; no more injustice; no more tears.

This vision of where ultimate wholeness can be found is an explicitly theological one, built on a Christian view of life that cannot easily be deduced from human nature and human experience. It is not even all that obvious to many people of faith. Many can see the limits of a life focused on earthly pleasures. Some can see the limits of a life focused on the quest for inner peace or good relationships. But to see that even eternal life in heaven with God is not the ultimate Christian hope requires a different way of rendering the very meaning of biblical faith.

My claim, and the claim of at least the strand of the Christian tradition that I represent, is that ultimately all the wholeness that we strive to experience for ourselves, even that of spending eternity in the presence of God, is best enfolded and taken up in a broader vision of God's purposes in the universe and on earth. The ultimate destination for God's work in the world is his kingdom, or reign, and so it must become our ultimate project as well. That's why Jesus taught his disciples to pray "Thy kingdom come, thy will be done, on earth as it is in heaven."

This version of the Christian hope is grounded in beliefs that I have articulated in various ways in this book and that go to the very core of the Christian faith. They are embedded in every Christian creed ever formulated and confessed:

There is one God, Creator of heaven and earth. This is God's world, and to God belongs rightful sovereignty over all creatures and all events.

While we do not know about other planets, we do know that God created free and responsible creatures on this one, and they misused that freedom and initiated a damaging rebellion against God that characterizes our existence as a species to this day. God is king, and yet we have rejected his reign. We are not what we were made to be, though poignant evidence of what we were made to be is still visible in all of us.

God could have chosen to abandon us to our own folly and sin. But people who believe that the biblical message is true believe that God has been involved in the redemption of human beings, the restoration of earthly community, and the renewing of the earth since immediately after we began to make a mess of it. This redemption reached its peak in Jesus Christ and will be concluded in the events that follow his return to earth.

According to the Scriptures, when Jesus returns, it will mean the final triumph of God over Satan and all forces of evil and an end to the misery that so afflicts human existence (Revelation 21:1–5). When Jesus "came preaching the good news of the kingdom" (Matthew 4:17), he was promising that his presence was inaugurating that reign. All who follow him work to advance God's reign day by day. We work for the kingdom even though we know that we do not know—just as our ancestors did not know—whether we will see its culmination in our own lifetimes. And so we wait for the day when Jesus returns to bring that work to completion.[2]

> *God's intent is to purge, heal, reclaim, and reconcile to himself the earth and its inhabitants, and this is what will occur at the end of time.*

Many Christians who know about the promise of Christ's return assume that the end of all things will involve a destruction of this earth and a transfer of God's people to heaven. So in the end their hope is not so much for the redemption of this world but for their personal escape from it in the company of other believers. They believe this based on their interpretation of certain key biblical passages, such as 2 Peter 3:9–10 and 1 Thessalonians 4:13–18.

I am among those who believe that although the details are not shared with us, what the Bible actually teaches is the final "renewal" of all things earthly, rather than their destruction. God's intent is to purge, heal, reclaim, and reconcile to himself the earth and its inhabitants, and this is what will occur at the end of time.[3] It does, sadly, appear to include the destruction of those who rebel against God without repentance. But its focus is the joyful reclamation of the earth and its inhabitants, who will be ruled by Christ the King. This theme links together such core biblical concepts as the Creation, the Fall, judgment, redemption, God's kingdom, and final consummation.

The biblical hope is not that we might escape from a decaying or destroyed earth but that we might have a share in a redeemed and renewed earth, when at last every tear shall be wiped away and all who enjoy a relationship with God shall do so forever. Our hope is not in an eternal disembodied state but in resurrection, sharing in the resurrection of our Lord Jesus Christ, as part of God's making all things new (Revelation 21:1–5).

When Christ returns, the resistance against God that has so permeated human experience will be broken at last, and life on earth will experience a dramatic transformation. This is what is meant by the kingdom of God. It is the triumph of God over all adversaries and adversarial forces and the peaceable reign of God in Christ over the earth as he now reigns in heaven (Matthew 6:10).

In this context, we can see that all legitimate hopes nurtured in the human heart find their proper place within the triumph of God. It is right to seek wholeness through personal moral renewal and a well-ordered, happy, and virtuous life. It is right to seek wholeness through reconciled relationships. It is right to seek wholeness through eternal union with God. In the time of the full triumph of God, all these fabulous blessings, and more, will finally characterize our experience. It's what we were designed for all along.

This vision of the kind of future that is coming also reveals the folly of accounts of human nature that do not include God or lives that are lived as if God does not exist. We see that ultimately our understanding of human nature and a good human life hinges on our view of the existence and character of God and God's project in relation to the earth.

The imprint of God's original design is still apparent enough in human nature that many stumble or grope part of the way toward this ultimate vision of human flourishing and the good life even without embracing the Christian faith. We have seen this as we have explored various aspects of human nature in this book. Christians are not alone among those who have discovered key truths about our nature.

In the end, though, the Christian faith offers a vision of what it means to be human that is ultimately rooted in its understanding of what it means to be God. Our nature and destiny find their meaning in light of the nature and destiny of the God who created us. It is impossible ultimately to embrace the Christian account of humanity without embracing the Christian account of God. When we do, we find that true wholeness in life's journey happens when God's hopes become our hopes and God's dreams become our dreams. When we live as if our dearest hope and most precious goal is to see God's will prevail, then we can truly understand the meaning of the Christian faith and can enjoy the blessings of a fully human life.

NOTES

CHAPTER ONE

1. Solomon Goldman, *In the Beginning* (1949), quoted in Ralph Woods (ed.), *The World Treasury of Religious Quotations* (New York: Garland Books, 1966), p. 359.
2. Alister McGrath, quoted in Mark Water (ed.), *The New Encyclopedia of Christian Quotations* (Grand Rapids, Mich.: Baker Books, 2000), p. 524.
3. Larry L. Rasmussen, *Earth Community, Earth Ethics* (Maryknoll, N.Y.: Orbis, 1996).
4. Sondra Wheeler, "Power, Trust and Reticence: Genetics and Christian Anthropology," in Ron Cole Turner (ed.), *New Conversations* (Cleveland: United Church Press, 2002).
5. Donald E. Brown, *Human Universals* (New York: McGraw-Hill, 1991).
6. Lady Mary Wortley Montagu, quoted in Robert Andrews (ed.), *Columbia Dictionary of Quotations* (New York: Columbia University Press, 1993), p. 424.
7. Josephus, quoted in Water, *New Encyclopedia of Christian Quotations,* p. 1125.
8. Lynn White Jr., "The Historical Roots of Our Ecologic Crisis," *Science,* March 10, 1967, pp. 1203–1207.

9. Robert N. Wennberg, *God, Humans, and Animals: An Invitation to Enlarge Our Moral Universe* (Grand Rapids, Mich.: Eerdmans, 2003).
10. Steven Pinker, *The Blank Slate: The Modern Denial of Human Nature* (New York: Penguin, 2002), p. 52.
11. Jose Ortega y Gasset, quoted in ibid., p. 24.
12. Oscar Wilde, "The Soul of Man Under Socialism" (1891), quoted in Andrews, *Columbia Dictionary of Quotations,* p. 424.
13. Pinker, *Blank Slate,* p. 41.
14. Ibid., p. 41.
15. Ibid., p. 52.
16. Quoted in Langdon Winner, "Resistance Is Futile: The Posthuman Condition and Its Advocates," in Harold W. Baillie and Timothy K. Casey (eds.), *Is Human Nature Obsolete? Genetics, Bioengineering, and the Future of the Human Condition* (Cambridge, Mass.: MIT Press, 2005), p. 392.
17. C. S. Lewis, *The Abolition of Man* (New York: Simon & Schuster, 1996), pp. 69–70 (emphasis in the original).

CHAPTER TWO

1. Quoted in Water, *New Encyclopedia of Christian Quotations,* p. 142.
2. Lactantius, quoted in Woods, *World Treasury of Religious Quotations,* pp. 572–573.
3. Basil the Great, quoted in Water, *New Encyclopedia of Christian Quotations,* p. 142.
4. Cyril of Alexandria, quoted in ibid., p. 972.
5. Gregory A. Boyd and Paul R. Eddy, *Across the Spectrum* (Grand Rapids, Mich.: Baker Books, 2002), p. 92.
6. Pinker, *Blank Slate,* p. 41.
7. Ibid., p. 50.
8. Ibid., p. 51.
9. Ibid., p. 58.
10. To make matters more complicated, it is also possible to interpret the New Testament as teaching that those who die

in Christ prior to the return of Christ enter into Christ's presence immediately in some intermediate spiritual state (Philippians 1:23). But the culminating act of salvation is clearly depicted as including a bodily resurrection, at least for those who have died in Christ.

11. *Catechism of the Catholic Church* (Liguori, Mo.: Liguori, 1994), p. 94, para. 368.

CHAPTER THREE

1. Catherine Keller, *From a Broken Web: Separation, Sexism, and Self* (Boston: Beacon Press, 1986), p. 166.
2. John Macmurray, quoted in Stanley J. Grenz, *The Social God and the Relational Self: A Trinitarian Theology of the* Imago Dei (Louisville, Ky.: Westminster/John Knox, 2001), p. 12.
3. Dietrich Bonhoeffer, *Letters and Papers from Prison* (New York: Collier Books, 1972), p. 105.
4. This section draws on my own *Getting Marriage Right* (Grand Rapids, Mich.: Baker Books, 2004), esp. ch. 3.
5. *Catechism of the Catholic Church*, p. 462, para. 1889.
6. Jürgen Moltmann, *History and the Triune God* (New York: Crossroad, 1992), p. 86.
7. The language comes from John D. Zizioulas, *Being as Communion* (Crestwood, N.Y.: Saint Vladimir's Seminary Press, 1985).

CHAPTER FOUR

1. See, for example, Jean Bethke Elshtain, *Who Are We? Critical Reflections and Hopeful Possibilities* (Grand Rapids, Mich.: Eerdmans, 2000). Elshtain's two main categories for discussing sin in this volume are as pride and as sloth.
2. The expression "ancestral shadow" comes from James Waller, *Becoming Evil: How Ordinary People Commit Genocide and Mass Killing* (New York: Oxford University Press, 2002), ch. 5. Even though Waller uses the expression to discuss human

evolutionary development and its legacy, it fits nicely with my argument here as well.

3. Aristotle, *Ethics* (New York: Penguin, 1976), p. 101.

4. Wendy Farley, *Tragic Vision and Divine Compassion: A Contemporary Theodicy* (Louisville, Ky.: Westminster/John Knox, 1990), p. 44.

5. Augustine, *On Free Will,* quoted in Woods, *World Treasury of Religious Quotations,* p. 931.

6. See especially Augustine, *Confessions,* bk. 3, trans. John K. Ryan (New York: Doubleday, 1960).

7. Aristotle, *Ethics,* pp. 63, 66.

8. For a nice discussion of this dimension of sin, see Cornelius Plantinga Jr., *Not the Way It's Supposed to Be: A Breviary of Sin* (Grand Rapids, Mich.: Eerdmans, 1995), ch. 7.

9. Augustine, *To Publicola,* quoted in Woods, *World Treasury of Religious Quotations,* p. 931.

CHAPTER FIVE

1. Those who find a strong view of divine control over events incompatible with human freedom are called, interestingly enough, incompatibilists. Those who think it is, or must be, possible to hold together both such great divine power and real human freedom are called compatibilists. Most orthodox Christians today hold some form of compatibilism because they want to affirm both divine sovereignty and human freedom and responsibility, as the Bible does.

2. John Calvin, *Institutes of the Christian Religion* (Louisville, Ky.: Westminster/John Knox, 1960), p. 201, 1.16.2.

3. For a brief and comprehensible overview of this very difficult issue, see Gregory A. Boyd and Paul R. Eddy, *Across the Spectrum: Understanding Issues in Evangelical Theology* (Grand Rapids, Mich.: Baker Books, 2002), ch. 2. In theological circles, it is most often called the sovereignty or divine providence debate.

4. A profound treatment offering a theology that takes Satan and the struggle against him seriously is presented in two volumes by Gregory A. Boyd: *God at War: The Bible and Spiritual Conflict* (Downers Grove, Ill.: Intervarsity Press, 1997) and *Satan and the Problem of Evil: Constructing a Trinitarian Warfare Theodicy* (Downers Grove, Ill.: Intervarsity Press, 2001).

5. John Calvin, quoted in Water, *New Encyclopedia of Christian Quotations,* p. 377.

6. Byron Curtis, quoted in ibid., p. 377.

7. *Catechism of the Catholic Church,* p. 445, paras. 1810–1811.

8. John Chrysostom, in Water, *New Encyclopedia of Christian Quotations,* p. 377.

9. For a nice discussion of the biblical understanding of freedom in contrast with modern notions, see Richard Bauckham, *God and the Crisis of Freedom: Biblical and Contemporary Perspectives* (Louisville, Ky.: Westminster/John Knox, 2002).

10. Philip Turner, *Men and Women: Sexual Ethics in Turbulent Times* (Cambridge, Mass.: Cowley, 1989), p. 15.

CHAPTER SIX

1. Mike Tyson, quoted in Tim Smith, "Battered Tyson Plots Return," *New York Daily News,* June 19, 2004 [http://www .nydailynews.com/news/gossip/story/204530p-176399c .html].

2. Dietrich Bonhoeffer, *The Cost of Discipleship* (New York: Simon & Schuster, 1937).

3. Luther emphasized the centrality of salvation coming as a gift of God to believers who receive that gift through grace; he did expect true Christians to live morally, but he was also quite pessimistic about the number of true Christians one could actually expect to find in the world. For a key essay that touches on these themes, see "The Freedom of a Christian," in John Dillenberger (ed.), *Martin Luther: Selections from His Writings* (New York: Anchor/Doubleday, 1961).

4. Bruce C. Birch and Larry L. Rasmussen, *Bible and Ethics in the Christian Life,* rev. ed. (Minneapolis, Minn.: Augsburg Fortress, 1989), p. 46.

5. Reinhold Niebuhr, *The Nature and Destiny of Man* (New York: Scribner, 1943), vol. 2, ch. 4.

6. This argument is made quite powerfully by Dallas Willard in *The Divine Conspiracy: Rediscovering Our Hidden Life in God* (San Francisco: HarperSanFrancisco, 1998).

7. All quotations are from *Catechism of the Catholic Church.*

8. See my *Righteous Gentiles of the Holocaust: Genocide and Moral Obligation,* 2nd ed. (Minneapolis, Minn.: Paragon House, 2003), ch. 5–6.

9. Birch and Rasmussen, *Bible and Ethics,* p. 74.

CHAPTER SEVEN

1. Jim Collins, *Good to Great: Why Some Companies Make the Leap to Greatness . . . and Others Don't* (New York: Harper-Collins, 2001).

2. Lewis B. Smedes, *A Pretty Good Person: What It Takes to Live with Courage, Gratitude, and Integrity* (New York: Harper-Collins, 1991).

3. Garth Lean, *God's Politician: William Wilberforce's Struggle to Abolish the Slave Trade and Reform the Morals of a Nation* (Colorado Springs, Colo.: Helmers & Howard, 1987).

4. William Wilberforce, quoted in ibid., pp. 54–55.

5. W.E.H. Leckey, quoted in ibid., p. 69.

6. Florence Nightingale, quoted in Basil Miller, *Florence Nightingale: The Lady of the Lamp* (Minneapolis, Minn.: Bethany House, 1975), pp. 47–48.

7. Val Webb, *Florence Nightingale: The Making of a Radical Theologian* (Saint Louis, Mo.: Chalice Press, 2002).

8. A lengthy excerpt from this book can be found in *Florence Nightingale: Letters and Reflections* (Evesham, England: James, 1996).

9. Debra Jensen, "Florence Nightingale's Mystic Vision and Social Action," *Scottish Journal of Religious Studies,* 1998, *19*(1), 71–72.

10. Miller, *Florence Nightingale,* p. 47.

11. A brief but excellent biography of Bonhoeffer is by Renate Wind, *Dietrich Bonhoeffer: A Spoke in the Wheel* (Grand Rapids, Mich.: Eerdmans, 1992).

12. John de Gruchy, "The Development of Bonhoeffer's Theology," in John de Gruchy (ed.), *Dietrich Bonhoeffer: Witness to Jesus Christ* (Minneapolis, Minn.: Augsburg Fortress, 1991), p. 1.

13. Geffrey B. Kelly and Burton Nelson (eds.), *Dietrich Bonhoeffer: A Testament to Freedom* (San Francisco: HarperSanFrancisco, 1995), p. 479.

14. *The Cost of Discipleship* (New York: SCM/Macmillan, 1959); *Letters and Papers from Prison,* ed. Eberhard Bethge (New York: SCM/Macmillan, 1971); *Ethics* (New York: SCM/ Macmillan, 1955). Many other books, and other editions of these books, can be found.

15. Dietrich Bonhoeffer, "Stations on the Road to Freedom," in *Letters and Papers from Prison,* p. 371.

16. Stephen B. Oates, *Let the Trumpet Sound: A Life of Martin Luther King Jr.* (New York: HarperCollins, 1994), pp. 88–89.

CHAPTER EIGHT

1. Aristotle, *Ethics,* p. 68.

2. This account of the kingdom of God is a much abbreviated version of what can be found in my *Kingdom Ethics: Following Jesus in Contemporary Context* (Downers Grove, Ill.: Intervarsity Press, 2003), written with Glen H. Stassen.

3. For relevant passages that support this claim, see Psalm 67:3–5; Isaiah 11:6–9, 35:1–10, 65:17–25; Matthew 6:9–13; John 1; Acts 3:21; Romans 8:18–23; Philippians 2:8–11; Hebrews 1; Colossians 1; Ephesians 1; and Revelation 1:5–7, 7:9–12, 22.

FURTHER READING

Augustine of Hippo. *The Confessions of Saint Augustine* (John K. Ryan, trans.). New York: Doubleday, 1960.

Baillie, Harold W., and Casey, Timothy K. (eds.). *Is Human Nature Obsolete? Genetics, Bioengineering, and the Future of the Human Condition.* Cambridge, Mass.: MIT Press, 2005.

Barbour, Ian G. *Nature, Human Nature, and God.* Minneapolis, Minn.: Augsburg Fortress, 2002.

Bauckham, Richard. *God and the Crisis of Freedom: Biblical and Contemporary Perspectives.* Louisville, Ky.: Westminster/John Knox, 2002.

Birch, Bruce C., and Rasmussen, Larry L. *Bible and Ethics in the Christian Life* (rev. expanded ed.). Minneapolis, Minn.: Augsburg Fortress, 1989.

Boyd, Gregory A. *God at War: The Bible and Spiritual Conflict.* Downers Grove, Ill.: Intervarsity Press, 1997.

Boyd, Gregory A. *Satan and the Problem of Evil: Constructing a Trinitarian Warfare Theodicy.* Downers Grove, Ill.: Intervarsity Press, 2001.

Brown, Donald E. *Human Universals.* New York: McGraw-Hill, 1991.

Brown, Warren S., Murphy, Nancey, and Malony, H. Newton (eds.). *Whatever Happened to the Soul? Scientific and Theological Portraits of Human Nature.* Minneapolis, Minn.: Augsburg Fortress, 1998.

Catechism of the Catholic Church. Liguori, Mo.: Liguori, 1994.

Clayton, Philip, and Schloss, Jeffrey (eds.). *Evolution and Ethics: Human Morality in Biological and Religious Perspective.* Grand Rapids, Mich.: Eerdmans, 2004.

Cooper, Terry D. *Sin, Pride, and Self-Acceptance: The Problem of Identity in Theology and Psychology.* Downers Grove, Ill.: Intervarsity Press, 2003.

Diamond, Jared. *The Third Chimpanzee: The Evolution and Future of the Human Animal.* New York: HarperCollins, 1992.

Elshtain, Jean Bethke. *Who Are We? Critical Reflections and Hopeful Possibilities.* Grand Rapids, Mich.: Eerdmans, 2000.

Farley, Wendy. *Tragic Vision and Divine Compassion: A Contemporary Theodicy* (Louisville, Ky.: Westminster/John Knox, 1990.

Fern, Richard L. *Nature, God, and Humanity: Envisioning an Ethics of Nature.* Cambridge: Cambridge University Press, 2003.

Flanagan, Owen. *The Problem of the Soul: Two Visions of Mind and How to Reconcile Them.* New York: Basic Books, 2002.

Fukuyama, Francis. *Our Posthuman Future: Consequences of the Biotechnology Revolution.* New York: Farrar, Straus & Giroux, 2002.

Gilligan, Carol. *In a Different Voice: Psychological Theory and Women's Development.* Cambridge, Mass.: Harvard University Press, 1982.

Glover, Jonathan. *Humanity: A Moral History of the Twentieth Century.* New Haven, Conn.: Yale University Press, 2000.

Grenz, Stanley J. *The Social God and the Relational Self: A Trinitarian Theology of the* Imago Dei. Louisville, Ky.: Westminster/John Knox, 2001.

Gunton, Colin E. *The Promise of Trinitarian Theology* (2nd ed.). Edinburgh: Clark, 1997.

Hefner, Philip. *The Human Factor: Evolution, Culture, and Religion.*
Minneapolis, Minn.: Augsburg Fortress, 1993.

Jeeves, Malcolm (ed.). *From Cells to Souls—and Beyond: Changing
Portraits of Human Nature.* Grand Rapids, Mich.: Eerdmans,
2004.

Jenson, Robert W. *On Thinking the Human: Resolutions of Difficult
Notions.* Grand Rapids, Mich.: Eerdmans, 2003.

Kass, Leon R. *Life, Liberty, and the Defense of Dignity: The Challenge
for Bioethics.* San Francisco: Encounter Books, 2002.

Keller, Catherine. *From a Broken Web: Separation, Sexism, and Self.*
Boston: Beacon Press, 1986.

Kilner, John F., Hook, C. Christopher, and Uustal, Diann B.
(eds.). *Cutting-Edge Bioethics: A Christian Exploration of
Technologies and Trends.* Grand Rapids, Mich.: Eerdmans, 2002.

Lean, Garth. *God's Politician: William Wilberforce's Struggle to Abolish
the Slave Trade and Reform the Morals of a Nation.* Colorado
Springs, Colo.: Helmers & Howard, 1987.

Lewis, C. S. *The Abolition of Man.* New York: Simon & Schuster,
1996.

Machuga, Ric. *In Defense of the Soul: What It Means to Be Human.*
Grand Rapids, Mich.: Brazos, 2002.

McFadyen, Alistair I. *The Call to Personhood: A Christian Theory of
the Individual in Social Relationships.* Cambridge: Cambridge
University Press, 1990.

McKibben, Bill. *Enough: Staying Human in an Engineered Age.*
New York: Henry Holt, 2003.

Moltmann, Jürgen. *God in Creation.* San Francisco: HarperSan-
Francisco, 1985.

Moreland, J. P., and Rae, Scott B. *Body and Soul: Human Nature
and the Crisis in Ethics.* Downers Grove, Ill.: Intervarsity Press,
2000.

Niebuhr, Reinhold. *The Nature and Destiny of Man,* Vol. 1: *Human
Nature,* and Vol. 2: *Human Destiny.* New York: Scribner, 1941,
1943.

Oates, Stephen B. *Let the Trumpet Sound: A Life of Martin Luther King Jr.* New York: HarperCollins, 1994.

Oden, Thomas C. *The Transforming Power of Grace.* Nashville, Tenn.: Abingdon Press, 1993.

Pasternak, Charles. *Quest: The Essence of Humanity.* Hoboken, N.J.: Wiley, 2003.

Peters, Ted. *Sin: Radical Evil in Soul and Society.* Grand Rapids, Mich.: Eerdmans, 1994.

Peterson, Anna L. *Being Human: Ethics, Environment, and Our Place in the World.* Berkeley: University of California Press, 2001.

Peterson, Gregory R. *Minding God: Theology and the Cognitive Sciences.* Minneapolis, Minn.: Augsburg Fortress, 2003.

Pinker, Steven. *The Blank Slate: The Modern Denial of Human Nature.* New York: Penguin Books, 2002.

Plantinga, Cornelius, Jr. *Not the Way It's Supposed to Be: A Breviary of Sin.* Grand Rapids, Mich.: Eerdmans, 1995.

Rasmussen, Larry L. *Earth Community, Earth Ethics.* Maryknoll, N.Y.: Orbis, 1996.

Rees, Martin. *Our Final Hour: A Scientist's Warning: How Terror, Error, and Environmental Disaster Threaten Humankind's Future in This Century—on Earth and Beyond.* New York: Basic Books, 2003.

Ruether, Rosemary Radford. *Sexism and God-Talk: Toward a Feminist Theology.* Boston: Beacon Press, 1983.

Sanders, John. *The God Who Risks: A Theology of Providence.* Downers Grove, Ill.: Intervarsity Press, 1998.

Shermer, Michael S. *The Science of Good and Evil: Why People Cheat, Gossip, Care, Share, and Follow the Golden Rule.* New York: Henry Holt, 2004.

Stassen, Glen H., and Gushee, David P. *Kingdom Ethics: Following Jesus in Contemporary Context.* Downers Grove, Ill.: Intervarsity Press, 2003.

Waller, James. *Becoming Evil: How Ordinary People Commit Genocide and Mass Killing.* New York: Oxford University Press, 2002.

Webb, Val. *Florence Nightingale: The Making of a Radical Theologian.*
    Saint Louis, Mo.: Chalice Press, 2002.
Wilson, James Q. *The Moral Sense.* New York: Free Press, 1993.
Wind, Renate. *Dietrich Bonhoeffer: A Spoke in the Wheel.* Grand
    Rapids, Mich.: Eerdmans, 1992.
Zizioulas, John D. *Being as Communion.* Crestwood, N.Y.: Saint
    Vladimir's Seminary Press, 1985.

THE AUTHOR

David P. Gushee is Graves Professor of Moral Philosophy and Senior Fellow, Carl F. H. Henry Center for Christian Leadership, at Union University. He has served for nine years at Union, a Tennessee Baptist college, after three years on the faculty of Southern Baptist Theological Seminary and three years on the staff of Evangelicals for Social Action. He earned his doctorate at the Union Theological Seminary in New York.

In addition to serving as a professor, Dr. Gushee preaches, counsels, lectures, and writes. His writing includes several dozen syndicated columns each year for Religion News Service and beliefnet.com and regular articles for *Christianity Today, Books and Culture,* and other magazines and journals. He is the author or editor of eight books, including *Kingdom Ethics: Following Jesus in Contemporary Context* (InterVarsity Press, 2003), written with Glen H. Stassen, which was named best theology or ethics book of the year by *Christianity Today* in 2004. His most recent book is *Getting Marriage Right: Realistic Counsel for Saving and Strengthening Relationships* (Baker, 2004).

Dr. Gushee and his wife, Jeanie, have been married twenty-one years and have four children. They live in the west Tennessee town of Jackson.

INDEX

217

Other Book of Interest

So Much More
An Invitation to
Christian Spirituality
Debra Rienstra
Cloth   ISBN: 0–7879–6887–0

"*So Much More* is a radiant manifesto for the fully realized Christian life. Rienstra speaks to the heart without mawkishness, speaks to the mind without logic-chopping, and speaks to the doubtful without patronizing. With good humor, and with erudition worn lightly, Rienstra provides a compelling Christian account of sin and grace, reason and revelation, the longing for God, the mystery of suffering, and the pathways of love and service."—*Carol Zaleski, professor of religion, Smith College*

What does it truly mean to live as a Christian? This intimate, engaging, and beautifully written book speaks to the heart of Christian faith and experience rather than to any one branch or theological position. Debra Rienstra weaves her own experiences as a Christian into chapters on central topics such as transcendence, prayer, churchgoing, the Bible, sin and salvation, and suffering. This is a book for people who don't have all the answers, those who are still thoughtfully considering the depth and breadth of their faith and would like an evocative and sympathetic companion to accompany them on their journey.

Debra Rienstra is a professor of English at Calvin College and the author of *Great with Child: Reflections on Faith, Fullness, and Becoming a Mother.* She lives in Grand Rapids, Michigan.

224

12252

LaVergne, TN USA
16 January 2011
212646LV00003B/97/P

9 780470 889619